NUGGETS

OF

ROMANCE

F. W. BOREHAM

John Broadbanks Publishing
Eureka, CA 2016

F. W. Boreham is one of the most gifted writers from any generation. I particularly love his biographical sketches. He makes me feel as if I am traveling back in time and personally meeting with my beloved heroes, great men and women of faith. Do yourself a favor and read every page of *Nuggets of Romance*.

Dr. Dave Park
Co-Author of *Stomping Out the Darkness* and *The Bondage Breaker-Youth Edition*

For several years now I've been blessed by the reissuing of F. W. Boreham's books by John Broadbanks Publishing. Now I'm all the more excited to see a collection of Boreham's essays that are for the first time in book form. These gems were part of a book Dr. Boreham was working on at the time of his death. I'm so glad we now have these precious last articles available to us through John Broadbanks Publishing.

Nick Harrison, author of *Magnificent Prayer, His Victorious Indwelling,* and *Power in the Promises*

F. W. Boreham had many extraordinary skills which made him an extraordinary man of God. Most people think of Boreham as a great preacher and writer. Queen Elizabeth II certainly did, which is why she honored him with the Order of the British Empire (O.B.E.) for Services to Preaching and Literature.

It is well-known among those who have come to know Boreham that his two preeminent skills are romance and story-telling. F. W. Boreham could see the romance in the ordinary and had a way of romancing his audience in the process. Boreham only wrote one biography, but after this he developed an amazing talent for incorporating biographical sketches in nearly all of his subsequent essays, which drew from these lives nuggets of insight and wisdom. This collection of later essays is thus aptly titled *Nuggets of Romance.*

I have benefited greatly as a pastor and preacher by reading the essays of Dr. F. W. Boreham, and I'm sure that you will too as you read this collection!

Dr. Andrew Corbett
Pastor of Legana Christian Church
www.fwboreham.com
Producer of *Navigating Strange Seas, The F. W. Boreham Documentary*

F. W. Boreham is Australia's most collectable religious author—and he deserves to be! (He's also collected widely elsewhere). It's wonderful that John Broadbanks Publishing is making his titles available to a 'generation that knew not Boreham!' I'll have to start collecting again!

Rev. Dr. Rowland Croucher,
Director, John Mark Ministries

Reading this magnificent collection of short essays by F.W. Boreham made me sad for so many moments spent reading something else. His prose is as rich and colorful as the characters his heart felt deserved memorializing. His casual insights are dazzling.

Steve Bell,
singer/songwriter

John Broadbanks Publishing
Eureka, CA
2016

Printed in the United States of America

ISBN: 978-0-9832875-5-1
eISBN: 978-0-9832875-7-5

Cover Design: Laura Zugzda
Layout: Marcia Breece

If the life of the ordinary person is a nugget of romance, what a literary goldmine the life of the extraordinary person should prove.

F. W. Boreham, *The Mercury*,
9 December 1933

PUBLISHED BY
John Broadbanks Publishing

F. W. Boreham
Second Thoughts –Introduction by Ravi Zacharias (2007)
A Packet of Surprises: The Best Essays and Sermons of F. W. Boreham (2008)
Angels, Palms and Fragrant Flowers: F. W. Boreham on C. H. Spurgeon (2009)
Lover of Life: F. W. Boreham's Tribute to His Mentor (Revised and Expanded) (2009)
All the Blessings of Life: The Best Stories of F. W. Boreham (Revised) (2010)
Loose Leaves: A Travel Journal (2010)
Loose Leaves eBook (2010)
All the Blessings of Life eBook (2010)
In Pastures Green: A Ramble through the Twenty-third Psalm (2011)
The Chalice of Life: Reflections on the Significant Stages in Life (Second Edition) (2012)
From England to Mosgiel (2012)
Lover of Life eBook (2013)
The Coming of Snowy (2015)
My Christmas Book (2015)

Geoff Pound
Making Life Decisions: Journey in Discernment (2009)
Talk About Thanksgiving: Stories of Gratitude (2010)
How F. W. Boreham Won the War of Words (2014)

Jeff Cranston
Happily Ever After: Studies in the Beatitudes (2010)

CONTENTS

Foreword...ix
A Cataract of Gossip...1
A Housewife's Triumph..5
A Mammoth Personality..10
A Scholar's Dream...15
A Stormy Petrel...20
Immensities of History..25
The Glory of Retreat..30
The Rationale of Journalism..................................35
Vindication of Patriotism......................................40
We Go to Press..45
A Golden Tradition..50
A Healing Minstrelsy...55
A Remunerative Investment...................................60
An Evangelist of Humanity...................................65
Creator of a Craft..69
Father Time's Makeweight.....................................73
Laureate of the West..80
Pastels of Sound..85
Rhetoric in Stone..90
The Lamps of Liberty..95
A Cheer for the Year..99
A Literary Calamity..102
A Study in Light and Shade..................................108
An Explosive Genius...113
An Unpredictable Scientist...................................118
First Across Australia...122
Imagination and Science.......................................126
Possibility Thinker...130
Sweetness and Light...135
The Integrity of Science..140
Volumes of Splendor..145
About the Cover...150
Publisher's Note...151

Foreword

These are some of the chapters from the book F. W. Boreham was writing at the time of his death. These essays were published in Australian newspapers over many years but in *Nuggets of Romance* they are brought together in a book for the first time.

These articles were written as editorials for Saturday newspapers not sermons for Sunday congregations. Dr. Boreham writes attractively and persuasively, as is evident in this opening line to one of his chapters: "Courage never shines so lustrously as when in full retreat." His writing gleams with bold and wise assertions, like this evocative statement: "Immensity is magnificent medicine."

Readers of this book will discover the secrets as to why F. W. Boreham is regarded as one of the greatest essayists. His love of communication and his itch to write are evident on every page. His style is vigorous, full of flourish and intriguing detail. He writes as if he is chatting with you before a crackling fire.

As in his earlier books, Frank Boreham often put his own ideas into the mouth of John Broadbanks, so his convictions are conveyed through many of the descriptions of his subjects. When writing about John Green, F. W. Boreham is conveying his own views about the recording of history:

> Green held that the historian needs the vivid imagination of the novelist; he needs the mathematical accuracy of the scientist; he needs the penetrating insight of the philosopher; and he needs the contemplative temper, the soulfulness, and the graceful diction of the poet.

While F. W. Boreham writes articles about journalism or the Bible, his main subject is people and real life. Many of his biographical editorials are about heroes who dazzled with their brilliance but Boreham also selects many 'minor characters,' 'second-rate poets,' 'first mates' and 'makeweights' to encourage his readers to see the best in lives that were mediocre and flawed.

Enjoy and treasure these 'nuggets of romance' from the literary goldmine of F. W. Boreham.

Dr. Geoff Pound
April 2016

A Cataract of Gossip

Somebody has said that there are two advantages in soliloquy. The man who talks to himself can be sure of hearing a sensible man talk, and he can be sure of having a sensible man to talk to.

The general principle obviously requires, according to circumstances, some modification, but, in the case of Oliver Wendell Holmes, it requires none at all. He was an excellent talker, and he never talked so well as when prattling away to himself. And, since it would have been a thousand pities for so much piquant and delicious wisdom to have been the monopoly of so very restricted an audience, Dr. Holmes rendered the world a notable service by placing his private chatter on permanent record.

Indeed, his real genius lay, not in making to himself such sagacious and penetrating observations but in embalming them so artlessly in the pages that he penned. In the hands of most men, his philosophizing would, on paper have become ponderous and unconsciously tedious. The babbling stream of irresponsible tittle-tattle would have been transformed into a wilderness of dreary metaphysics.

But the ingenuity of Dr. Holmes in inventing the breakfast table, and in making the landlady and her boarders say the things that, in reality, he had been saying to himself, preserves his chatter as unadulterated chatter, and, incidentally, gives it universal and abiding appeal.

Literature Enters Upon a New Phase

Oliver Wendell Holmes was a dapper little man, standing barely five feet three, of slight figure, upright bearing, meticulous attire, sprightly stride, clean-shaven face, a friendly smile, and twinkling eyes that seemed to miss nothing visible.

After toying with the idea of following his father into the ministry, he applied himself to the study of law, and finished up by becoming a doctor. The rest of his life he divided into four parts. He spent three years as a general practitioner; became, for two years, professor of anatomy at Dartmouth; returned to a practice at Boston for six years; and then became, for 35 years, professor of anatomy at Harvard. It was during this last period that all his literary work was done.

And it was well done. He struck an entirely new vein. His one claim to immortality rests on the breakfast table books—*The Autocrat*, *The Poet* and *The Professor at the Breakfast Table*. Each volume is a cataract of chatter, and, divested of the artistry by which the conversation is attributed to all sorts of fictitious characters who are supposed to surround the famous table, the chatter simply represents the self-communings of Oliver Wendell Holmes. He is all the while gossiping away to himself.

He will always be remembered as the most charming egotist that the republic of letters has ever known. He was not crushingly, overwhelmingly egotistical like Johnson; he was not satirically, bitingly egotistical like Coleridge; he was genially, vivaciously, magnetically egotistical in a way that was all his own. He liked to hear himself talk; and, in contrast with some conversationalists possessed of that dubious propensity, he made his chatter irresistibly delightful to his listeners.

Genial Master of a Thousand

He wields an extraordinary magic. He somehow contrives to bind his reader to himself with hoops of steel. You feel that you are in a comfortable armchair on one side of a cheerful fire, and that he is in the armchair facing you; and it never so much as occurs to you that the conversation is entirely a one-sided affair.

Or, to change the simile for one of his own, he regarded each reader almost amorously. "It is," he says, "like going for an arm-in-arm walk in the moonlight." Who can resist the fascinating guile of such an egotist? He may prattle of shoes or ships or sealing-wax; we are all ears. He may ramble on about cabbages or kings; we sit entranced at his feet. Herein lies the art—the entirely novel and original and intriguing art—of Oliver Wendell Holmes.

Since the world began, no author has dealt with so many separate themes as the creator of *The Autocrat*. He does it without the slightest attempt to appear learned or imposing. He flits from subject to subject as lightly and as daintily as a butterfly flits from flower to flower. He knows exactly how long to pause at each point. Moreover, his moods are as varied as his topic. He is always philosophical; he is often informative; his disquisitions are frequently suffused with humor; they are sometimes touched with irony; and there are passages in which the pathos is so pronounced that tears are at no great distance.

Altogether, he is one of the most engaging figures in our literature and his admirers will grasp with avidity the excuse that an anniversary offers to sample afresh his appetizing wares.

A Housewife's Triumph

Just a century ago a busy little mother published a book that, scribbled in odd moments snatched from her many children and her many chores, was soon selling by the million. Before very long, too, *Uncle Tom's Cabin* had been translated into forty languages, had precipitated a civil war and had shattered the shackles of the slaves.

The most vivid description of Mrs. Harriet Beecher Stowe is her own. "I am a little bit of a woman, somewhat more than forty," she says, "just as thin and dry as a pinch of snuff; never very much to look at in my best days and very much used-up by now." She had spent her life in an atmosphere in which the theology was inexorable, the drudgery illimitable, the finances infinitesimal, and the children innumerable.

She produced her masterpiece soon after the birth of her seventh child. She used to say that she was always glad when the time for her accouchement came, because it gave her an excuse for going to bed for a week or two and enjoying a delicious rest. As the children entered the home in quick succession, the financial problem became desperate. Was there any way of augmenting her husband's slender income? Her fingers had always itched to write.

Defying the multiplicity of her domestic duties, she resolved to make the attempt. She produced a thin little volume of stories that did little or nothing to relieve the strained economy of the home and that gave little or no promise of better things to come. But a crisis followed, and, with the crisis, came a challenge that awoke a sensitive soul to grandeur and greatness.

Stirred by the Sight of Slavery

Born in 1811, Harriet Beecher Stowe was a minister's daughter; she herself married a minister, and she had six brothers in the ministry. She proclaimed these facts for all they were worth whenever she heard it affirmed, as it often was, that the churches looked with approbation, or at least with tolerance, upon slavery. "I ought to know," she would retort, "and, indeed, I do know; you may take it from me that the churches hate slavery like poison!" There were exceptions, of course, but, generally speaking, her contention was sound.

Her mother died when Hatty was only a few weeks old. While she was still a toddler, her father married again. The lady impressed everybody by her sense, beauty, and charm. Hatty fell in love with her as soon as they were introduced; but some mysterious instinct in her baby breast revolted against the relationship between her father and this attractive intruder. "All right!" she exclaimed, while this strange mood was upon her, "you married my daddy; when I grow up I'll marry yours!"

In 1832, the year in which Hatty came of age, her father was made president of Lane Theological Seminary in Cincinnati, and, four years later, she married one of the professors on his staff. Cincinnati is separated only by a narrow waterway from Kentucky. Whenever she crossed that barrier, Hatty had the opportunity of witnessing the horrors of slavery. She said little at the time, but she was stung to the quick by the indignities to which the colored girls were exposed, by the way in which members of families were torn from each other by the auctioneer's hammer, and by the callous cruelty of the marketeers. She even helped some of the slaves to escape.

The idea that the whole iniquitous traffic might be abolished, root and branch, and that she herself might become a potent instrument in its destruction, never entered Hatty's head until a sister-in-law wrote a letter that changed the course of history.

A Spark Kindles a Huge Conflagration

If, this lady said, if she possessed Hatty's literary gift, she would write a book that would stir the whole nation to a recognition of the evils of slavery. Mrs. Stowe rose from her chair, clasping the letter in her hand. Pacing the floor for a moment, she suddenly turned to those about her, to whom she had read the letter aloud. "I will!" she exclaimed, "I will."

And, as all the world knows, she did. The book was written on all sorts of scraps of paper in odd moments that could be snatched from making beds, cooking meals, mending socks, and washing babies. Between the beginning of a sentence and its close she was sometimes interrupted three or four times by pressing household duties. But she contrived to finish the herculean task at last and nobody was more amazed than she at its phenomenal success.

For that success was both immediate and overwhelming. On the day of its publication, 3,000 copies were sold; within a year 300,000 had been demanded, and the numbers soon ran into millions.

Uncle Tom was dramatized and played in first-class theaters all over the world. For the first time in her life, Mrs. Stowe was lifted above pecuniary anxiety although the wealth that surprised her was but a fraction of what it would have been had her rights been properly secured. The most eminent literary figures in both hemispheres smothered her with congratulations. Abraham Lincoln referred to her as "the little lady who made the big war." Whittier addressed an ode:

> To her, who, in our evil time,
> Dragged into light the nation's crime
> With strength beyond the strength of men,
> And, mightier than their swords, her pen.
> To her who worldwide entrance gave
> To the log-cabin of the slave.

In England she was welcomed by Queen Victoria and was feted everywhere. She blinked like an owl in the glare. Following her husband's death in 1886, she spent the last ten years of her long life in pensive retirement at Hartford, the home of her girlhood, delighting above everything else in winning the affection of people who had never so much as heard of Uncle Tom.

A Mammoth Personality

London little knew what was in store for it when, on March 2, 1737, a young man, Samuel Johnson by name, who had recently married a widow more than twenty years older than himself, set out for the metropolis to try his luck. Carlyle called him the greatest soul in all England, a giant, invincible soul. Johnson is one of the most familiar figures in all history. Thanks mainly to Boswell's vivid and palpitating pages, "the old philosopher is among us in the rusty coat with the metal buttons and the shirt which ought to be at wash, blinking, puffing, rolling his head, drumming with his fingers, tearing his meat like a tiger and swallowing his tea in oceans. No human being who has been so long in his grave is so well known to us." Thus Macaulay, who adds that we have but to open Boswell's unique and immortal volume and, as if by magic, the whole of that coffee-club drama unrolls color before us. Judge Johnson by any standard you will, he is a really Homeric figure, good as he is great.

For, in the most pitiful days of his poverty, his purse—for what it was worth—was always at the disposal of his still poorer friends. And look at this!

It is one of Boswell's records thrown into dainty verse by Robert Brough:

> When this goodly man was old
> On a night so wet and cold,
> As towards his home he strolled,
> He espied in the bitter London street
> Lying, drenched with rain and sleet,
> A poor girl with naked feet
> Who had died in the cruel, cruel cold,
> If this sage, so worn and old,
> Had by accident not strolled
> Where she lay. He was torn by illness' wrack,
> His old joints were fit to crack,
> But he bore her on his back safe away.

And Brough concludes the poem, a fairly long one, by describing the way in which, at the funeral at Westminster Abbey, derelicts and deadbeats Johnson had helped insisted on taking their places among the principal mourners.

Gentleness Subsisted with Rugged Exterior

Was there ever such an asylum of ne'er-do-wells as that house in Gough Square? It was, as Macaulay says, the home of the most extraordinary assemblage of social flotsam and jetsam ever brought together. They were at constant war with one another and with poor Frank, Johnson's servant. Sometimes they even turned savagely upon their benefactor himself, whining and complaining so persistently that Johnson was glad to shuffle off to the Mitre Tavern to evade them. He often wished that they were as responsive and appreciative as his pets. Towards these he behaved with a solicitude that almost amounted to chivalry. He insisted on going himself to buy the cat's food lest Frank, should feel himself degraded by being required to wait upon an animal, or lest, being put to the trouble, he should conceive a dislike to the poor creature! "Few men on record," says Carlyle, "have had a more merciful, tenderly affectionate nature than old Samuel: within that shaggy exterior of his there beat a heart warm as a mother's, soft as a little child's." And Sir Leslie Stephen avers that, of all the heroes, statesmen, philanthropists, and poets who sleep in Westminster Abbey, there are few whom, when all has been said, we can love as heartily as Samuel Johnson. Like all sensible men, the doctor dearly loved to be praised honestly, but he would have desired no tribute more eloquent than that.

He may not have been a saint of the conventional type, but he was a man of the finest devotion. He was a tremendous believer in the Bible, and in prayer. He read as many chapters of the Bible each day as would ensure his completing the entire Book once a year. He loved the Church of England Prayer Book and sometimes thought of collecting the best prayers in the language and gathering them into one comprehensive volume.

But when his friends pressed him to put the design into execution, he pleaded he was unworthy of so sacred a task. Mrs. Thrale, in her *Anecdotes*, says that Johnson could never recite that majestic Latin hymn, the *Dies Irae*, without bursting into tears. And who can forget that famous scene at the Literary Club when, one of the members, chancing to quote a verse from the 19th Psalm, Johnson instantly caught fire, snatched off his hat, and with most impressive solemnity, repeated the whole of Addison's noble paraphrase of that stately psalm?

People Live Forever in the Lives They Inspire

Johnson's place in literature is difficult to define. In one way it cannot be regarded as a dominant place, for who reads him? He is in the extraordinary position that his reputation rests, not on anything he himself wrote, but on a book an incomparably inferior man wrote about him. Lord Rosebery used to say that, apart from one or two poems and one or two biographical sketches, Johnson never penned anything worthy of perusal. And yet, like Socrates among the philosophers, he is a most commanding and authoritative figure in English letters. In this respect he stands in striking contrast to Shakespeare. We revel in Shakespeare's writings and like to memorize them, but we never bother our heads about the man. In Johnson's case, we display the utmost avidity in regard to the person but know next to nothing of what he wrote.

A great spirit often does his best work, not in his own proper person but by means of the disciples who, arising under the magnetism of their personality, do what they themselves could never have done. Johnson appeared at a moment when the genius of English literature seemed dead. It was a time of unparalleled sterility. Yet Johnson was scarcely laid in his honored grave when there arose a multitude of minstrels so great that when, shortly afterwards, the Poet Laureate died, the Government of the day found itself embarrassed by such a wealth of riches that it knew not whom to appoint. Johnson was a strong man whose immense energy and conviction held other minds in thrall, a man who ruled without making any conscious attempt to do so. While his work remains unread, on the highest and dustiest shelves, he himself still lives, and as long as English letters last his fingerprint will be seen on every page.

A Scholar's Dream

Many people will want to honor the memory of John Richard Green, one of the most scholarly, one of the most painstaking, one of the most artistic, and one of the most engaging of British historians. In the year of Queen Victoria's accession, Green was born at Oxford. Few men owe so much to their birthplace as did he. From earliest infancy he became saturated in the university atmosphere. His childish eyes stared in wondering awe at the pageant of academic life moving around him. As soon as he was old enough to interest himself in such matters, the storied stones of the imposing old city began to whisper into his enchanted ear their hoarded secrets. Nothing delighted him more than to sit at the feet of very old men and women while they narrated to him the earliest happenings of which their memories preserved any impression.

The past to him was fairyland: he loved to plunge into its bewitching realms whenever the shadow of an opportunity presented itself. Any new discovery concerning some long-forgotten yesterday threw him into transports of excitement. He once won a valuable prize; but the volume itself seemed to possess no attraction for him: the thing that took his breath away was the fact that the gentleman who had placed it in his hands had, as a boy, gazed into the face of Dr. Johnson! Then, at the age of sixteen, he fell under the spell of Gibbon. The *Decline and Fall* swept the responsive and impressionable youth completely off his feet. The glamor of Gibbon fascinated him. It was a revelation to him of the conquests awaiting the historian who really understands his business. Delving more and more deeply into the picturesque territory that bygone ages offer to the fancy, Green became convinced that very few of the classical historians had cherished any adequate conception of the sublime potentialities of their craft. Lacking that rose-tinted vision, they had committed the unpardonable sin: they had actually made history dull.

Bringing the Dead Past to Life Again

Green held that the historian needs the vivid imagination of the novelist; he needs the mathematical accuracy of the scientist; he needs the penetrating insight of the philosopher; and he needs the contemplative temper, the soulfulness, and the graceful diction of the poet. It is because so few of those who have assumed the role of the chronicler have been able to command this wealthy equipment that most of their ponderous and pretentious volumes are allowed to lie in undisturbed repose upon our top most shelves. Since they themselves are so unconscionably arid and dry, we mercifully allow the cobwebs to enfold them. It is a case of dust to dust. Green argued that it serves them right. To him, history represented everything that was romantic, everything that was colorful, everything that was dramatic. In contemplating the stately and palpitating Past, he felt that he was watching an imposing and magnificent procession, a procession that, with gay banners waving and stirring music playing, was marching in splendid panoply and perfectly marshaled pageantry before his wondering eyes. If only somebody with eyes anointed and with soul on fire, could erect his easel, spread his canvas, arrange his pigments, and, with consummate artistry, immortalize its glory!

It was at the age of thirty-two that Green offered the hospitality of his heart to a lofty aspiration. It came to him like a dazzling dream and he gravely doubted the possibility of his giving to that noble ideal a concrete expression. If only he could write the history of his own people as that history had never before been written. It should be, not a history of our British wars, nor a history of our British kings, but primarily and essentially and fundamentally a history of our British people. He resolved that his production should never sink to the level of a drum-and-trumpet history. For anybody who cares to look back will recognize that, until Green ushered in the new vogue, a history of England was almost exclusively a recital of military campaigns and a piquant narrative of royal amours.

A Dreamer's Race with Death

Green vowed that, at any cost, he would write a history which should be a record of the great processes by which the nation had been built up. But, just as he had shaken himself free from all distracting entanglements, and had piled around his desk the notes that he had amassed in the course of his researches, he discovered to his dismay that his lungs were in ruins and that he might at any time drop into a consumptive's grave. However, Alexander Macmillan, of the famous publishing house, offered him £350 for the unwritten manuscript, with a promise of more if the book should be successful. Taking fresh heart from such encouragement, Green applied himself to the task that had fired his fancy and challenged his powers; and his crazy lungs notwithstanding, he lived to hear, five years later, the plaudits that greeted the publication of his book.

Better still, he lived to see his masterpiece enthroned as one of our English classics and to draw royalties on the sale of 150,000 copies. Then the curtain fell. Having permitted him to quaff this intoxicating goblet of triumph, the pitiless disease which his iron will seemed to have held at bay until his work was done, asserted its grim supremacy, driving him to the south of France, where in 1883, at the age of forty-six, he passed away. "I know what they will say," he exclaimed one day as, book in hand, he surveyed the grove of palms beneath his sickroom window. "They will say of me that 'he died learning.'" And those who today pay pilgrimage to his honored tomb at Mentone, within sight of the blue waters of the Mediterranean, will find those three words inscribed upon the monument that marks his grassy grave.

Stormy Petrel

William Cobbett, was made to mount the whirlwind and to ride the storm. Mountainous in form and volcanic in temperament, he presents for our contemplation the most arresting combination of pugnacity and polish of which we have any record. Upon Cobbett's burly figure, resolute features and robust character, John Leech is said to have based his familiar delineation of John Bull. Throughout the whole of his tempestuous and colorful career, William Cobbett certainly exhibited the massive masculinity that we invariably associate with that traditional personage. He called a spade a spade, and did it in immaculate English. His penetrating thrusts brought upon his towering head the venomous maledictions of highly placed and influential foes; yet his transparent honesty of purpose and his downright goodness of heart compelled the admiration and affection of the very men who squirmed beneath his vigorous assaults.

In his championship of the common people, Cobbett knew what he was talking about. The grandson of a farm laborer and the son of a small farmer, he was compelled to earn his own living as soon as he was six. He was out in the fields before it was light every morning, and, at night, he could scarcely struggle home. It was then, after a scanty meal had been hurriedly swallowed, that the books were brought out, and, with the father as schoolmaster, the business of education tackled. When the boys fell asleep over their lessons, as they often did, they were sent off to bed in disgrace. Those, Cobbett said later, were happy days. But since it was not good that such exacting conditions should continue, he dedicated the best efforts of his life to their amelioration.

A Story of Prisons' and Palaces

At the age of 17, Cobbett set out for London, arriving in the metropolis with exactly half a crown in his pocket. City life, however, was little to his taste. He decided to join the Marines; but, filling in the wrong form, was surprised to find himself a soldier of the King in the 54th Foot Regiment, under orders to sail for Canada. During his early years in the army, he devoted all his time and thought to the process of self-improvement. Unable to afford lamps or candles, he frequently read and wrote by firelight. He often had to study amidst the songs and shouts of the other members of his regiment. Yet no man in the barracks was more popular and everybody was sorry when he returned to England.

Cobbett plunged into the placidities of English life like a bull charging into a china shop. It soon became clear that, during years of intensive study, he had acquired a literary style that was the natural expression of his electric personality. He knew how to make every sentence sting. He called himself Peter Porcupine and the pseudonym was by no means misleading. His criticisms of 18th Century England were so caustic, and yet so tellingly phrased, that the entire populace was compelled to listen. Defying all the conventions, and cherishing a fine scorn of personal consequence, he soon found himself wading through seas of trouble. Mulcted in fines that involved him in bankruptcy, and flung into gaol for years at a stretch, he spent a large slice of his life in fleeing from England to America and then from America to England again. He was, however, no iconoclast. With prophetic eye he saw the things that needed doing and he was determined that they should be done. His stark sincerity attracted the ear of the King, while men like Pitt, Peel, and Windham were compelled to pay attention. He entered Parliament in 1830, and mellowing with the years, won for his cause a respect that, in his more violent days, had been denied him.

The Gentleness that Subsists with Force

For all his vehemence and bluster, there dwelt in Cobbett a surprising wealth of tenderness. His love story is as beautiful as any idyll. After three years of service with his regiment in Canada, he was out one winter morning before break of day. In an outhouse that he passed, he saw a girl busy with the washing. The snow was deep on the ground; the cold was piercing; it was still dark; yet she sang at her suds. "That's the girl for me!" Cobbett said to himself. Observing her more carefully he recognized her as an artilleryman's daughter to whom he had been introduced a day or two earlier. Cultivating her closer acquaintance, two difficulties presented themselves. She was only 13, and her father's regiment had been ordered back to England. During the years that followed, he wrote her regularly, and, fearful lest she should ruin her beauty by too much toil, he sent her all the money he could scrape together, a hundred and fifty guineas in all.

When Cobbett himself returned to the Homeland a few years later he found her a maid-of-all-work, earning two shillings a week. She smilingly accepted his proposal of marriage, and, at the same time, handed him a parcel which contained the entire sum that he had sent her. To the end of his days he never tired of singing her praises as a wife and as a mother. Nor was his devotion merely a matter of words. In one of his essays he urges husbands to demonstrate their fondness for their wives, not by endearing epithets, but by real understanding and practical sympathy. When on one occasion, Mrs. Cobbett was in delicate health, and, because of the barking of dogs, found sleep elusive, Cobbett slipped quietly out of the house, and, barefooted, lest she should hear his steps, spent the night driving the dogs to a distance. Cobbett represents one of those gigantic and enigmatic figures that make up the piquant charm of history. He had great faults, but they were faults of the head, never of the heart. He loved the English people, the English language, and the English home and he will always be remembered as a strong man and a good one.

Immensities of History

It was on March 7, 1804 that the British and Foreign Bible Society was founded. The churches naturally noticed the event on the anniversary; but, in this respect, there is no reason why the churches should have things all to themselves. The Bible concerns us all. No single factor has had more to do with the creation of our literature, with the molding of our legislation, and with the determination of our way of life. The minstrelsy of all the world's poets is rooted in the work of these ancient seers and singers; the statutes of all civilized peoples are based on the inflexible mandates of the Mosaic code; while all the chivalries and courtesies of life are the natural expression in human conduct of these immemorial ethics and ideals.

Immensity is magnificent medicine; that is one reason why our doctors send us to the seaside. We forget the tiny in the contemplation of the tremendous; we lose life's shallow worries in the vision of immeasurable expanses and unfathomable depths. "I loved to walk until I could see the open water," exclaims the baffled and frustrated Mark Rutherford. "The sea was a corrective to the littleness all around me." When we miss a train, or mislay a letter, or find a social program spoiled by rain, it exercises a steadying effect upon the nerves to reflect that Orion and the Pleiades still roll, Niagara still flows, Mt. Everest still wraps his clouds about him, daring a conqueror to tread his summit. The big things are as the big things always were.

The Evolution of a Perfect Language

The Bible richly deserves its place among these monumental immensities. In a sense it grows greater with the passage of the years. When the graybeards of today were in their cradles, the Scriptures had been translated into about two hundred languages; today they are published in a thousand. It is, indeed, not only great; it is infectious in its greatness; it imparts stateliness and splendor to everything it touches. The three periods of human history with which it stands most intimately related have come to be recognized as three of the most momentous eras that our little world has known. They represent the Rise of Greek Culture, the Renaissance in Europe, and the Evangelical Revival of the 18th Century. One may search the archives of mankind from the dawn of creation to this very hour without unearthing records that can put these three classical periods to shame. And each of the three finds its enduring monument in the existence of the sacred volume that the churches will magnify on Bible Sunday.

Dean Alford, perhaps the outstanding authority on the subject, declares that one of the most arresting coincidences of all time is the evolution of the Greek tongue during the years immediately preceding the Christian era. In the fairest portion of the south of Europe, amidst the indented coasts and rocky valleys and snow-clad ranges of Greece, there grew to perfection, Alford says, the most beautiful, fluent, and powerful language that ever flowed from the tongues of man. Among the brilliant intellectuals of Athens it received its edge and polish. In it, as in no other tongue known to men, the most minute turns of human thought found expression. Truths requiring almost microscopic mental discernment were exquisitely conveyed by it. It was a precision instrument of the finest possible quality. And, to add to its charms, it was an attractive and melodious language, charming the ear with its liquid music as well as gratifying the mind by its philological subtlety. Spread across the world by the conquests of Alexander the Great, himself a pupil of Aristotle and a writer of renown, humanity found itself in possession of a perfect vehicle for its thought at the very moment at which the most startling revelation of all time was about to be made.

The World Assumes a New Complexion

The European Renaissance transfigured the lives of all nations, including our own. In those days as Sir Sidney Lee avers, English people breathed a new atmosphere. They came, he says, under a new stimulus, compounded of many elements, each of them inspiring, almost intoxicating. New continents had been discovered, new oceans sighted. The entire atlas had been recast; the world had assumed an entirely new shape. Astronomy had been born again; new inventions had revolutionized commerce and industry. It was a regeneration of the human intellect. Men felt a passion for extending the limits of knowledge. In this welter of reconstruction, two movements, each supplementary to the other, stand out conspicuously. The one is Caxton's epoch-making introduction of printing; the other is Tyndale's translation of the Bible into the English language. The immensity of the volume became the natural reflection of the immensity of the age.

The third of these magnificences of history was the great evangelical revival that, in the 18th Century, exercised an influence so overwhelming, so dynamic and so irresistible that it transformed, fundamentally and permanently, every phase of our national life. In days when ancient thrones were tottering and hoary institutions crumbling, it preserved for us, as Lecky has shown, our national integrity and respect. Men saw the affairs of this world, and of every other, in a new perspective. In the sweep of this mountainous and memorable movement, all our great missionary societies sprang into being and a desire was created to give every man living a copy of the Scriptures in his own tongue. As a result, millions of tons of Bibles, in hundreds of grotesque and apparently fantastic languages, were shipped and borne to every lonely rock and remote oasis on which humans had made their abode. The sheer vastness of such an achievement possesses a tonic value for workers in every field of humanitarian enterprise and the churches are thoroughly justified in recounting, so notable an exploit.

The Glory of Retreat

Courage never shines so lustrously as when in full retreat. A dramatic and brilliant charge is a soul-stirring affair; but in the nature of things, few of us are permitted to cover ourselves with glory under such exciting circumstances. But we have our compensations. For, every day of our lives, we find ourselves under the necessity of executing a retreat. In the genial glow of fireside conversation we assume positions that, as the controversy develops, we see to be untenable; in the rush and bustle of life we say and do things that, on leisurely reflection, we sincerely regret; in waves of enthusiasm or in gusts of sudden indignation we commit ourselves to courses that, in the hush of twilight, we see to be tactless and futile; we even commit ourselves in writing to statements that we subsequently discover to be unjustifiable. These are the situations that provide most of us with the opportunity of displaying genuine gallantry. It is by the skill with which we extricate ourselves from such positions that we achieve distinction.

A coward never retreats. Having once taken up a position, he clings desperately to it, although he grimly feels that its occupation must be their ultimate undoing. "What I have written, I have written," exclaims Pilate, with an assumption of boldness, even while, in the profundities of his soul, a thousand voices are crying out in protest, and he secretly wishes that he had never put his hand to the fatal documents. Pilate is by no means alone. We have all heard of the politician who, finding himself in doubt as to one of the planks of his party's platform, yet dreading the displeasure of his leaders and associates, makes a bolder statement of his policy than ever and assures himself that he is once more on firm ground. He assumes a note of emphasis to cloak his torments of uncertainty. In his "Everlasting Mercy," our Poet Laureate, Mr. John Masefield betrays a flash of profound psychological and spiritual insight in making Saul Kane blaspheme more loudly, and offend more blatantly, after becoming the subject of deep religious convictions. It is the recoil of the soul from the thought of self-repudiation. It is, on the grand scale, the behavior of the boy who whistles to keep his courage up.

The Dream of Confessing Oneself Mistaken

In his "Water Babies," Charles Kingsley has familiarized us with the learned Professor Pllhmllusprt. In an extraordinarily able treatise, read at the annual meetings of the British Association held in Melbourne in 1899, the brilliant professor had demonstrated, to the utmost bounds of finality, that such a thing as a waterbaby did not exist, never had existed and never could exist. Shortly afterwards, however, when he and little Ellie were paddling about at the seaside, a real live waterbaby became entangled in Ellie's handnet! The professor's first impulse was to keep it; to name it after himself; and to brag of his remarkable discovery. But what would the British Association say? He therefore released it and invented a lot of long Latin words with which to explain it. "Now," adds Kingsley, "if he had told Ellie frankly that it was a waterbaby and that its unexpected emergence showed how easily the most honest and diligent students of nature may reach a false conclusion, she would have believed him implicitly, respected him still more deeply and loved him better than she had ever done before." But the poor little professor lacked the pluck. He was too great a coward to retreat. And so he missed his one and only chance of adding a deathless luster to his name.

The Passion of Science for Truth

In the course of his presidential address before the British Association, Sir Michael Foster outlined the qualifications that represent the two essentials of a distinctively scientific spirit. The first is absolute truthfulness: the other is moral courage. Professor Pllhmllusprt possessed neither. A true scientist, like Darwin, possesses both. Darwin would spend years in patient investigation, gathering data for the work in which he proposed to elaborate and demonstrate his theory, and then toss the entire work into the flames on being convinced that, in spite of all the evidence that supported it, the theory was fundamentally false. His son has told us how, on retiring for the night after a pleasant evening by the fireside, he could not sleep if he remembered having made a statement, however casual or immaterial, that was not absolutely in accord with the actual facts. He would even rise, long after midnight, to confess the slip into which his tongue had innocently betrayed him.

Grant Allen bears similar testimony to Sir Charles Lyell. All through the years, he taught a certain interpretation of the universe. Then, towards the end, new light dawned upon him. He saw clearly that his lifelong view was a false one. Should he therefore repudiate all that he had taught, and condemn the books that, with such care, he had written? The temptation to silence was tremendous. But his best self conquered. "Science," says Grant Allen, "has no more pathetic figure than that of the old philosopher, in his 66th year, throwing himself with all the eagerness of youth into the task of wrecking the very foundations of his beloved creed. But he did it. Deep as was the pang that the recantation cost him, he retracted his earlier works and accepted the theory that he had always rejected." Grant Allen's phrase is reminiscent of the apostolic statement concerning one who "now preaches the faith that he once labored to destroy." And, indeed, what is the process of conversion of which all the churches speak but a courageous turning of one's back upon the life that one deplores and a turning of one's face towards the ideal that beckons? It is a retreat, but a retreat that is invested with a glory all its own.

The Rationale of Journalism

It was on the eleventh in March 1702 that the first British daily newspaper made its appearance. Entitled "The Daily Courant," and produced by Master E. Mallet over against the Ditch at Fleet Bridge, the venture struck everybody as very much of a novelty. It consisted of a single page of two columns; and, in its initial issue, the publisher assured his readers that the journal would consist exclusively of news. He would not dare, he assured them, to make any comments of his own, since other people were as well qualified as he was to form their own conclusions. From that day to this, few departments of life can show a more striking process of evolution than that presented to our contemplation by the history of journalism.

Probing to the heart of things, a particularly interesting question arises. How are we to account for our insatiable appetite for news? A man comes home from the office glad to have left the cares of the world behind him. He enjoys a good dinner, and then, surrounded by the members of his family, he settles down to an evening by the fire. And the first thing that he does in the course of his evening's felicity is to open a journal, or listen to the radio, and thus involve himself once more in the whirl of those affairs that, an hour or two earlier, he had found it such a relief to forsake. Or, in the summer, he goes for his annual holiday. He carefully selects a spot so secluded that nothing of life's fret and fever can possibly disturb the tranquillity of his retirement. Yet, once there, the great event of the day is the arrival of the newspaper. He looks forward to its coming with greater eagerness, and abandons himself to its contents with keener zest, than he has ever done in the ordinary work-a-day life at home.

Ampler Gregarianism of Humanity

In days of public excitement a man tears open his paper to learn the latest developments of the portentous matter that is agitating the universal mind. In days of unruffled serenity, when everything is as calm as the proverbial millpond and life resolves itself into one prolonged yawn, he vaguely feels that the newspaper may contain a thrill that will invest a humdrum existence with a new glamour of interest, and scans its columns with a curiosity and an avidity peculiar to periods of uneventfulness. But whatever the temper of the time, and whatever the state of society at the moment, man wants his paper and won't be happy till he gets it. One wonders why. Why do the people of the smallest and most remote settlements want the news? Why cannot Diggers Gully be satisfied with Diggers Gully?

Why cannot Horseshoe Creek be content with Horseshoe Creek? Why should they bother their heads about the great wide world?

Nothing of the kind is to be seen beyond the bounds of humanity. No creature of the wilds betrays any solicitude concerning the fates or fortunes of other creatures at a distance. But man must have the news, for, unlike all other animals, he is conscious of a life infinitely larger than the life of the individual. He cherishes a gregarianism of an ampler kind than the fields and the forests know. Wolves may go in packs, birds in flocks, and deer in herds; but the life of each of these aggregations is independent of the life of each similar company. The pack binds a few wolves in one, but there is no tie that embraces universal wolfhood. Each man, however, feels that all men belong to him. Each isolated township feels itself to be part and parcel of every distant city. The individual wants the world, and his yearning for the world expresses itself in his everlasting thirst for news.

Life Without, Stimulates Life Within

This ravenous craving is one of the sublimest things about us. It is humanity's master passion. In his classical narrative of the emotion and excitement amidst which he at last found Livingstone, Stanley says that the one thing for which the lost explorer clamored was the news. Stanley urged him to read his letters. "No, no," cried Livingstone, "the letters can wait a few minutes longer; tell me the news! How's the world getting on?" Then, buried in that dense African jungle, the two men sat for hours, while the one told the other of all the elections, the revolutions, the wars, the assassinations, the inventions, and the countless transformations that had overtaken the world while the lost man had been buried in the dark continent. Livingstone became a changed man. Fresh tides of vitality rushed into his frame; his haggard face shone with enthusiasm. "You have brought me new life!" he murmured repeatedly.

The incident is extraordinarily revealing. A man wants the world; a geographical fragment will not satisfy them; a hemisphere is not enough. A man may live in a hut or a humpy at the back of the bush, or at the other end of nowhere; but he will hunger for a cluster of far-off continents, and the romance of ten thousand distant islands. Stanley poured the world into the starved soul of Livingstone, and every fiber of his being tingled with new animation. A man's hunger for the world is a pulsation of the infinity, which stirs within us. "Thou hast set the world in their hearts," declares an ancient prophet. "God so loved the world . . .," the best known text in the Bible affirms. That being so, it is small wonder that man, made in his Maker's image, should share the same all-embracing and cosmopolitan passion. Nor, in view of man's rapacity for news, is it any wonder that Dr. Weymouth and all the later translators should have discarded the medieval word "gospel" in favor of its modern equivalent "good news." They speak of the good news of the love of God and the redemption of Christ; and that, as Tennyson observed in one of his beautiful love letters to Emily Sellwood, is the latest and greatest and best news of all.

Vindication of Patriotism

In his lifetime, Giuseppe Mazzini was hunted from pillar to post, expelled from one country after another, imprisoned and degraded, reduced to starvation and driven to the verge of suicide; yet, a few years after his death, his name was most revered where at one time it had been most abhorred. The tide turned very quickly. In his *Italica*, William Roscoe Thayer points out that, as soon as Mazzini died, his foes conceded his eminence. Those who had execrated him as a monster hailed him as a martyr. "The wise instinct of the world," says Mr. Thayer, "has long since admitted Mazzini into the company of its really great men. He would certainly be included in any group of ten outstanding representatives of the nineteenth century." This is lofty praise, as anyone will discover who attempts to compile a list of the ten mightiest spirits of the age in which Mazzini figured. Yet nobody who has carefully taken the measure of the man will feel inclined to challenge Mr. Thayer's dictum.

Mazzini holds the admiration of thoughtful men on many grounds, but, conspicuously among these, stand the clarity of his ideal and the fidelity with which he pursued it. He saw his goal as plainly at sixteen as he did at sixty, and he never for a moment swerved from his determination to achieve it. No country in the world has been more loved than Italy, and no Italian has loved Italy more devotedly than Mazzini. Yet he was not, in the ordinary sense, a political agitator. He had every sympathy with those who strove to increase wages, reduce prices, and generally, to improve the lot of their fellowmen. But he never disguised from himself the fact that such reforms would not ameliorate the conditions that he deplored or hasten the consummation for which he incessantly labored. He was not concerned, he said, about the cost of corn and cabbages. "What I do care for is that Italy shall be great and good, fulfilling the splendor of her mission in the world." He was no iconoclast, no breaker of idols, no reckless destroyer. He was a rebel, it is true, but he was the most constructive rebel that Europe has ever known.

Truth for Ever on the Scaffold, Yet—

He was, moreover, a rebel by means of whose rebellion every country in the world has been enriched. He smashed a few windows, but he only smashed them to let a little fresh air into the stuffy atmosphere that, in his time, all the nations were breathing. An intense admirer of Dante, he was profoundly impressed by Dante's combination of purest poetry with practical patriotism. He gloried in the way in which Dante sweetened and sublimated the life of Italy, and, modeling himself on so classic a master, he set himself to do in the nineteenth century what the illustrious Florentine had done in the fourteenth. This was his ideal; did he realise it? Up to the time of his death there was little evidence of his having done so. There were times in which his pitiful failure unnerved him and he seriously doubted the justice of his cause. Had he any justification for prompting good men to suffer and die for a dream that seemed chimerical? As he reflected on the stalwarts who had laid down their lives in following him, and of the women and children desolated by their deaths, he felt, he tells us, like a criminal, and was filled with a terrible remorse. The only comfort that he could find at such times lay in the fact that he was seeking no guerdon for himself. He had nothing to gain and everything to lose by adhering to his self-imposed program.

If his comrades suffered, so did he. He was thrown into prison, and, later driven from the country under the threat of a disgraceful death if he dared to return. Austria, France, and Switzerland denied him hospitality. Go where he would, he was harried by the authorities. The Marchesa Rice Pareto Magliano some time ago contributed to the *Contemporary Review* a memory of her childhood. Mazzini, a fugitive under sentence of death, sought refuge in her father's home. One afternoon they saw a posse of police approaching. "Mazzini took from his pocket a bundle of the tiny missives which he was always writing—the little sheets by which his teachings were propagated—and gave them to my mother, who slipped them into her bodice. He then rushed to his hiding-place, a box in the ironing room. The housemaid, who was ironing, conceived the ingenious idea of arranging on the box one of my father's starched shirts. The police searched the house in vain." The incident is typical of the phase in his experience through which he was then passing.

Condemned in Life, but Crowned In Death

An outcast in Europe, London was, of course open to him, and to London he went. But he says that the "hell of exile" on the Continent was never so dreary as his life in the English capital. His poverty was of the most disgusting and degrading kind. He was compelled to herd with the lowest of the low, and on Saturdays would often pawn the clothes off his back to buy enough food to carry him over the weekend. Margaret Fuller describes him as prematurely old; all the vital juices seemed exhausted; his eyes were bloodshot; his skin orange; flesh he had none; his hair was mixed with white; his hand was painful to touch. At last, assuming the name of Giorgie Brown, he crept back to Italy to die.

His funeral was the first indication of the impression he had made. Eighty thousand people followed his body to the grave. Even his opponents began to realize that there was something reasonable and lofty in his contentions. The heresies of one generation often become the orthodoxies of the next. Never was this exemplified so strikingly as in the case of Mazzini.

Cities that had threatened him with death if he dared to enter their boundaries, erected statues to his memory. A new crop of orators and authors echoed his sentiments and won world-wide applause by uttering truths that had brought him to noisome dungeons. Fifty years after his death the nations that had exiled and banished him vied with each other in heaping their tributes on his honored name.

We Go to Press

I t was on the first of March, in the old city of Bruges, that William Caxton began the work that was to transform the world. No man knows exactly when he was born. We like to think that, like an actor who has been hiding in the wings and suddenly steps into the limelight, William Caxton emerged, on world history. No man did more than he to give shape and color to our modern civilization; of no man's personal history do we know less. But, on that day in 1438, he became apprenticed to Robert Large, a citizen of enormous wealth and immense authority, who, a few months later, celebrated with extraordinary splendor his election to the office of Lord Mayor of London. Amid the pomp and circumstance that attended his master's elevation, we catch the first glimpse of the man who taught Englishmen to print. During the years that followed he spent a good deal of his time in Flanders as governor of the English Guild of Merchant Adventurers; but, whatever his position and whatever his duties, he was secretly cogitating the reform with which his name is inseparably associated.

It seems almost incredible today, when we discuss the literary triumphs of the Middle Ages, that the books that we so familiarly mention were originally published in handwritten script. Obviously, literature could never be popular under such conditions. Only the wealthy could afford a scroll or even purchase the right of perusal. Caxton held that earth's loftiest thought should be available to earth's lowliest citizens. During his residence on the Continent, he came upon a number of literary treasures that he ardently coveted for his own people. He set to work to copy them. The venture, heart-breaking in its sheer immensity, excites both wonder and admiration. Imagine a reversion to 15th century conditions. Imagine a young Australian going to London and finding, at the British Museum, the manuscripts of *David Copperfield*, *Pendennis*, *Ivanhoe* and *Adam Bede*. Imagine his setting to work to make accurate and neatly written copies of these manuscripts in order that his Australian friends may share with him the delight that they have found in their perusal.

Labor-saving Par Excellence

By this frolic of fancy we are able to appreciate the courage that constitutes Caxton's first claim upon our veneration. The strain was terrific. "In all this writing," he says, "my pen is worn; my hand weary; my eyes dimmed by overmuch concentration on the white paper; my courage is failing; while old age creepeth on me daily, enfeebling all my body." Necessity was ever the mother of invention, and it was out of the necessity imposed upon him by his insufferable weariness that Caxton's most memorable work was born. Tired to death of copying the endless folios, it occurred to him that there must be adventitious and mechanical aids to so exhausting an undertaking. He soon found that there were. They were extremely primitive, extremely clumsy, extremely costly, and extremely slow. But Caxton's imaginative genius and practical sagacity saw in these crude beginnings the protoplasmic germ of an epoch-making reform. He bought a ramshackle old press; returned excitedly to England; and was soon able to announce that any man who wanted to buy a book should come to the Sign of the Red Sale "where he should have it good and cheap." The Sign of the Red Sale was, curiously enough, within the precincts of Westminster Abbey. The innovation startled England. Learned men, fashionable women, and great nobles thronged the little printing house to see how the miracle was performed, while less intelligent people declined to go near it, declaring that such results could only be achieved by commerce with evil spirits. For 14 years Caxton was able to continue his toils; the business went ahead by leaps and bounds. Books became so cheap that most people could afford to buy them, and, in order that they might enjoy the pleasures offered, thousands of people learned to read who had never before felt any desire for that accomplishment.

Harbinger of a New Dawn

The printing press startled the world at the very moment at which the world had something worth printing. The air tingled with sensation and romance. It was an age of thrills. Civilization was being overhauled and recast. The very planet was being recreated. Going east and west, the great navigators were finding new continents and new islands everywhere. It was, too, the age of the renaissance. Men were eager to think. Astronomy was being born. In the realms of philosophy, music, art and science, illustrious adventurers whose names will live forever, appeared like bright stars that twinkle suddenly out of the age-long dark. An infinite horizon was opened to the simplest minds. Men fell in love with the universe. Moreover, with that revived interest in ancient culture, there awoke in the minds of the people an insatiable desire to possess the Scriptures in their own tongue. And, at that psychological moment, William Tyndale arose. A private tutor in Gloucestershire, he conceived the idea of making the simplest ploughboy as familiar with the Scriptures as the most erudite scholars then were. As a result, he completed his monumental translation in such a masterly way that, except in matters of detail, no subsequent revisers have been able to improve on his majestic production. The people had obtained what they wanted. Caxton's presses scattered the copies broadcast over the country, and all our historians have borne eloquent witness to the important part played by this notable development in fashioning our modern way of life. The rise of Caxton, therefore, was not only an epoch-making event; it was a glowing portent. It was the symbol of the dawn of an era without parallel in history. The man who would discover and demonstrate Caxton's contribution to human progress must establish a contrast between the past five centuries and the five centuries that immediately preceded them.

A Golden Tradition

In view of the sensational strides that surgery has taken in recent years, it is eminently fitting that we should offer our homage to the illustrious memory of Lord Lister. It is scarcely an exaggeration to say that the history of surgery divides itself into two epochs—before Lister, and after. In the old days, as Tyndall put it, "we were scourged by invisible throngs, attacked by impenetrable ambuscades, and it was only under the leadership of Lister that the light of science was thrown upon the murderous dominion of our foes." The brave story represents one of our classical romances.

With no traditions to suggest such a destiny or move him in that direction, Lister resolved, when quite a child, to be a surgeon. None of his relatives were attached to the medical profession, and it is doubtful if the boy had ever spoken to a doctor in his life. He was adamant, however, and never for a moment swerved from his early purpose. As soon as he entered his 'teens he began to macerate the bones and articulate the skeleton of every creature he could lay his hands upon. His parents, Quakers of the old school, viewed his grim propensities with feelings akin to horror. His father was proud of the boy's penchant for scientific research, but he shook his head gravely at the ideas of his son becoming a surgeon.

Surgery the Handmaid of Nature

For what, after all, does the antiseptic doctrine amount to? If we forsake for the nonce the technical and academic terminology of the schools, and reduce the matter to the common parlance of the street and the fireside, it simply means that Pasteur in France and Lister in England aroused the medical fraternity to a recognition of the fact that, favorable conditions having been secured, Nature itself is the supreme healer. It is not the business of the surgeon to heal, but to obtain for Nature those conditions for which it imperatively stipulates. Any surgeon will confess that it is not in his power to heal a wound. The wound must heal itself. His duty consists in keeping it so immune from foreign substances, and so free from malignant bacteria, that the injured limb gets a fair chance of compassing its own restoration. Some vague hints of all this had been detected, and their significance suspected, away back in medieval times. But it was reserved for Lister to read the secret rightly and to transform our schools of surgery by giving it practical demonstration and effect. The work was slow, but he never lost heart and never looked back, and, in a way of which he never even dared to dream, he came into his own at the end.

Within the memory of men still living, Lister stood, with his back to the wall, fighting as a man fights for his life on behalf of that new conception of surgery with which his name will always be associated. He fought, not as a pugilist, but as a knight. There was a winsomeness and a chivalry about his engaging personality that completely disarmed his critics and opponents. He was absolutely sure of his ground, and he exhibited his confidence, not in noisy bluster, but in quiet strength. W. E. Henley, the poet and the friend of Robert Louis Stevenson, was once operated upon by Lister. Acknowledging his indebtedness to the distinguished surgeon who had thus saved his life, Henley said that "his rare, wise smile was sweet with certainties." The exquisite phrase reflects, as eloquently as mere words can do it, the calm and gracious poise of Lister's mind.

Laurels that were Late, but Luxurious

At the time of Lister's advent, the situation was desperate. Doctors stood appalled at their own helplessness. The stars in their courses seemed to be fighting against them. Disease was spread by the very people who were seeking most assiduously to cure it. Surgeons carried contagion from patient to patient; nurses bore it from bed to bed on their aprons, bandages, and sponges. To sentence a patient to an operation was like signing his death warrant. Lister was worried to the point of distraction. He resolved to probe the problem to its very heart. As a result, he came to a sensational conclusion. The whole trouble, he announced, was— dirt! So, to the elimination of dirt, in every shape and form, he applied his stately powers. His new crusade awoke a storm of opposition. At the meetings of the British Association held at Leeds in 1869, Lister was roundly charged with arrant stupidity. Four years later, the *Lancet* warned the entire profession against him. At Edinburgh, Professor Caird, then a student, was solemnly adjured to have nothing whatever to do with him. The fierce campaign lasted until 1877, Lister being then 50. In that year the tide turned.

Lister was made Professor of Clinical Surgery at King's College Hospital. Almost immediately, his former enemies rallied to his side. Sir James Paget recanted and frankly withdrew earlier strictures. "I look back with shame," Sir James declared, "on that part of my life." In 1883, Lister was made a baronet, and, in 1897 was raised to the peerage. It was the first occasion on which a member of the medical fraternity had been so honored. At the Coronation of King Edward the Seventh, Lister was made a Privy Councillor. "What pleased me far more than the honor," he said, "was the fact that the King shook hands with me, and said that, but for me, he could not have lived to wear the crown." Lister died in 1912. A grave in Westminster Abbey was offered, and declined, but a noble monument perpetuates his memory there. Men of such a mold are the glory, not only of a nation, but of all mankind; and it is fitting that, on every suitable occasion, we should recall their heroic achievements and acknowledge the incalculable debt under which they have placed us.

A Healing Minstrelsy

If, today, the British and American peoples find themselves bound together by the most intimate and most sacred ties, their amity is largely the fruit of the fine work of James Russell Lowell. In his time Lowell was a personality to be reckoned with. Handsome in appearance, brilliant in conversation, and of infinite geniality and charm, he became at once the central figure in any social group that he chose to adorn. W. M. Rossetti said of him that he had a cast of countenance that would have graced an Italian saint or a medieval troubadour, and that the painter who, wishing to portray the rejuvenated Faust or Goethe, could have persuaded Lowell to pose for his model, would have been very fortunate indeed.

Theodore Watts-Dunton once finely said of Lowell that, though literature was the passion of his life, he knew that to join the hands of England and America, as he set himself to do, was to make a poem in action— a poem that would work towards the final emancipation of the English-speaking race, the final emancipation of the world. In view of all that has happened of recent years these words seem almost prophetic, as do the lines

addressed to the British and American peoples at the
time of Lowell's death:

> Your hands he joined—those fratricidal hands,
> Once trembling each to seize a brother's throat,
> How shall ye honor him whose spirit stands
> Between you still? Keep love's bright sails afloat
> For Lowell's sake, where once ye strove and smote
> On those wide waters that divide your strands.

It was to achieve this historic triumph that Lowell
made the greatest sacrifice of his career.

The Poet who Became a Plenipotentiary

For, to enable him to realize his dream, he had to
pay the price. The bald fact is that Lowell had it in him
to become a first-class poet yet never did become one.
Diplomacy shared with Poesy the hospitalities of his
soul and the Muses resented the divided devotion. As it
is, he may be described rather as an ethical rhymer than
as a classical poet. As he grew to maturity he recognized
the defects of his earlier work, but by that time he was
no longer so passionately in love with the laurels as to
apply himself diligently to the perfection of his latent
powers. As a natural consequence, he seldom rises
above an elaborate mediocrity. He says what he wishes
to say, and says it effectively, but he never says it with
the genius of a laureate, the rapture of a minstrel, or
the sweetness of a poet. Edgar Allan Poe once told him

bluntly that, while he was capable of work unequalled in the Western hemisphere, he was only turning out compositions that were essentially loose, ill-conceived and feebly executed, remarkable only for their obvious lack of literary finish.

His most intoxicating draught of fame came to him, strangely enough, as a result of the verses that he had published anonymously. As a protest against the Mexican War, and as a plea for the abolition of slavery, Lowell sent forth the Biglow Papers. Couched in the quaintest colloquialisms, and peppered with the choicest morsels of Yankee diction, the whimsical verses immediately captured the popular ear. "Who is Hosea Biglow?" everybody was asking. Lowell himself was constantly entangled in the discussion. "I found the Biglow jingles copied everywhere," he says. "I saw them pinned up in workshops; I heard them quoted and their authorship debated; and once, when rumor had at length drawn my name into one of its eddies, I even had the satisfaction of hearing it demonstrated, in the pauses of a concert, that I was utterly incompetent to have written anything of the kind." It is at least a suggestive indication of what might have been had he wholeheartedly devoted his cunning to his craft.

Literary Renown Sacrificed

But he dissipated his brilliance. Invited by the President to go to Russia as Ambassador, Lowell declined on the ground that he owed something to the gifts that had lifted him from obscurity to eminence. Three years later, however, he accepted an appointment to the Court at Madrid, which led, in due course to his preferment as United States Ambassador to Great Britain. And thus, in a whirl of diplomatic duties and social functions, his literary gift was suffocated. He carried in his breast a divided heart. As a result, he never rises to super excellence. If, by a feat of concentration that should have been well within his power, he had focused his really amazing faculties upon any one of the imposing tasks to which he set his hand, his name would have shone with an even brighter luster and he would have taken his place among the greatest of the great.

He richly deserves, however, to be gratefully and admiringly remembered. By his facile pen and his enormous personal influence he turned the faces of two great nations towards each other. He therefore stands, as one of our historians has vividly said, a golden link between two worlds. In all his work he strikes, clearly, sanely and attractively, the purely ethical note. To him, life's ultimate issues were crystal clear. "Once," he sang:

> Once to every man and nation comes the moment to decide,
>
> In the strife of truth with falsehood, for the good or evil side;
>
> Careless seems the great avenger; history's pages but record
>
> One death-grapple in the darkness 'twixt old systems and the word;

Truth for ever on the scaffold, wrong for ever on the throne.

Yet that scaffold sways the future, and, behind the dim unknown

Standeth God within the shadow, keeping watch above His own.

In that fine faith he lived and labored alike in the literary and in the diplomatic fields. It was a real torture to him that, between the two great branches of the Anglo-Saxon world, no love was lost. He observed with genuine and growing sorrow the evidences of estrangement and alienation between his own people and the people of the British Isles. He regarded it as his supreme mission in life to heal that hurt, and the world owes him a heavy debt of obligation for the fidelity with which, to the last day of his life, he held faithfully to his exalted purpose.

A Remunerative Investment

It is just a hundred years since Dr. Thomas Guthrie startled the saints, the scholars, and the sobersides of Scotland by declaring that the waifs and strays of the Cowgate and the Canongate were as well worth saving as the daintily-dressed children of the Edinburgh West End. He soon proved by a practical experiment that the reclamation of the ragamuffins was not only a valuable item in the program of social reform, but a sound financial proposition into the bargain. Mr. Gladstone always felt that Guthrie represented the most perfect combination of passionate evangelism and practical philanthropy of which he enjoyed any experience. The work that Guthrie did in Scotland stands for all time as a conclusive demonstration of the principle that it is infinitely better to build a fence round the top of a precipice than to provide an ambulance at the bottom. Guthrie himself regarded the money spent upon his work as a particularly remunerative gilt-edged investment. By the most incontestable statistics he proved that the saving to the public purse in penal and charitable expenditure more than offset the cost of his institutions.

Rugged in appearance, massive in figure, and billowy in eloquence, Thomas Guthrie was a typical representative of the best life of Scotland in that day. The twelfth child in a family of thirteen, he inherited from parents of superb character and robust piety, a profound reverence for his country's history and traditions. He loved to describe his first school. The teacher was a weaver who plied his shuttle while he instructed his pupils. The schoolroom was the weaver's workroom, sitting room and bedroom. The loom occupied one corner, a bed stood in the second, another bed monopolized the third, and a table graced the fourth.

Determination Overcomes Initial Failure

Having set his heart on the ministry, Guthrie completed his divinity course only to find himself "a stickit minister." Not a church would look at him. Resolved, however, to allow no grass to grow under his feet, he filled in the long period of waiting, first by taking a medical course, then by serving for a year or two in a bank and, finally, by running a farm. Later on, at the pinnacle of his great renown, he found all three of these attainments extremely useful, although, as he sometimes pointed out with a smile, they had their drawbacks. One busy evening, for example, when every moment was precious, a woman was shown into his study. Guthrie prepared himself for a poignant story of spiritual dereliction or emotional distress. But when she came to the point, his visitor explained that, as he had the reputation for raising the finest calves in the country, she would be very grateful if he would tell her his secret.

When he did at long last find a pulpit opened to him in his own native Forfarshire, his colorful rhetoric and his novel methods soon created a sensation, with the result that, eight years later, he was summoned to Old Greyfriars in Edinburgh. For a while, he was wretchedly homesick. Standing, one gloomy afternoon, on George the Fourth Bridge, looking down on the squalor, the filth, and the misery of the Cowgate, he felt appalled and paralyzed by the stark horror of it all. Everything was foul, loathsome, revolting; the very smell of it sickened him. He mentally contrasted this with his old parish, with its singing larks, its daisied pastures, its decent peasants, its silvery streams, and the great blue sea rolling its lines of breakers on the sparkling shore. All at once a hand was laid on his shoulder, and, turning he found himself confronting the leonine head and finely-chiselled face of Dr. Chalmers. To his surprise, Chalmers congratulated him on the golden opportunity presented by his hideous environment. The unexpected words stirred him like a bugle-call and he determined on the spot to accept the challenge that Chalmers had suggested.

Humanity in Terms of Finance

He applied himself to the artistry of preaching with such success that his church was soon crowded to the doors. The poorest of the poor delighted in his ministry, while, as his reputation spread, men like Gladstone, Ruskin, Lord John Russell, Lord Macaulay, and others figured in his congregation. He soon received overtures from the finest churches in the land, but nothing would lure him from Old Greyfriars. The longer he lived in the city, however, the more impressed he became by the fact that all around him swarmed tens of thousands of children who had never been given a chance. Circumstances beyond their control had marked them for a life of crime. While still in the forties, Guthrie made his historic plea in their behalf. He founded schools at which the most destitute and abandoned city Arabs were taught, fed, clothed, and given vocational training.

The result exceeded his most sanguine expectations. Pointing to five hundred of his protégés, he claimed that if they had been allowed to drift into lives of vice and crime, they would have cost the nation £150,000. Shaped by his schools, their economic value was £200,000. So the country was making gold by the wagon-load, while, in addition, the children were being transformed and uplifted.

Guthrie died on February 23, 1873. Thirty thousand people followed the casket to its resting place in the Grange Cemetery. The children of his schools sang beside the grave. Among the eloquent tributes offered by the most eminent people of his day, Prof. John Stuart Blackie described him as:

A fine, strong-breasted, fervid-hearted man,
Who from dark dens redeemed, and haunts of
sin,

The city waifs, the loose, unfathered clan,
With prouder triumph than when wondering
Rome

Went forth, all eyes, to bring great Caesar home.

Among the stalwarts of the nineteenth century there are few greater than he.

An Evangelist of Humanity

Victor Hugo was a faggot of thunderbolts. His works represent a catalog of thrills. In many ways he stands unequalled. At the age of 15 he wrote poetry that would have won for him the most coveted distinctions of the French Academy if the Academy could have brought itself to believe that the boy actually penned the poems. As a child, sightless and voiceless, he seemed too frail to live. How could such a weakling have produced such epics? He was 28 when he published *The Hunchback of Notre Dame*, and he persisted along his path of excellence until, at 60, he wrote *Les Miserables*. Such consistence and persistence is altogether phenomenal.

His countrymen claim for him that he is the greatest master of romance that the world has ever seen, and that no man ever stirred the inmost heart of the French people as did he. But he did far more than this. Every treader of foreign fiction knows that the crucial test of authorship is the test of translation. Very few writers ever get translated into foreign tongues. Of those few, only a microscopic fraction become really popular on alien shores. But Victor Hugo holds the distinction of having written, in his native French, three novels—*Les Miserables*, *Travailleurs de la Mer*, and *Notre Dame*—which are as familiar throughout the Anglo-Saxon world as any three romances penned by an English writer.

A Philosopher Stands at the Heart of the Storm

In order to assess the value of this extraordinary tribute, it is only necessary to recall the amazing wealth of imaginative genius of which all the European nations, particularly our own, found themselves possessed during the 19th century. A mere list of the names represents a dazzling galaxy of brilliance; it follows, therefore, that to have attained superexcellence in such brave company is to have triumphed on a singularly lordly scale. Moreover, we have to remember that Victor Hugo's romances were written not with pen and ink, but with blood and tears. His life story is one long and tragic adventure. In his day everybody knew him. In those electrical and tumultuous times, he himself cut a striking and dynamic figure. Theophile Gautier has embedded his commanding features and expressive countenance in an exquisite cameo that will live imperishably.

To see Victor Hugo once was, Gautier says, to remember him vividly through all the succeeding years. He had a forehead rising like some marble monument above the serene and earnest countenance. Framing this splendid brow was a wreath of rich chestnut hair, falling to a considerable length behind. The face was closely shaven, and its exceptional pallor was relieved by a pair of hazel eyes, keen as an eagle's. His attire was neat and faultless—black frock coat, grey trousers, and small turn-down collar with an ample bow-tie. Here, in a few deft and graphic touches, the work of a master hand, Gautier has penciled for us, the man who stood with calm face and unflinching heart, amidst the social turmoil that seemed to be incessantly raging around him, and who refused to recognize defeat in the ostracism and loneliness of his later years. Few records are more moving than the records of those days in which he was eating out his heart in exile. He surrounded himself with all things beautiful; yet his banishment maddened him. On the day his wife's body was borne away to Paris for burial, he was forbidden by the authorities to accompany it. He bowed his head in grief, but his soul remained adamant, dauntless, indomitable. His own sufferings lend significance to his philosophy of life.

The Novelist Becomes the Seer

For Victor Hugo was essentially and preeminently a man with a message. In all his novels he portrays the foulest creatures imaginable, and shows that they may be uplifted and ennobled. "The multitude can be sublimated," he confidently declares. "These bare feet, these shivering forms, these shades of ignorance, these depths of abjectness, these abysses of gloom may be employed in the conquest of the ideal. This lowly sand which you trample beneath your feet, if you cast it into the furnace, may become resplendent crystals; by means of the lenses that it makes a Galileo and a Newton shall discover stars." Mr. W. T. Stead used to say that *Les Miserables* is the supreme novel of pity. "It is," he says, "the very gospel of compassion, written by an evangelist of humanity. Here we have the wrongs of the wretched sung as never before by one who unites the tenderness of a Christian with the passion of a revolutionist." What, it may be asked, is the secret of this pity and this passion?

It is, of course, rooted in faith. Victor Hugo looked, quite literally, not on the things that are seen, but on the things that are unseen. In cruel exile, writhing under the most ruthless and inexorable injustice, he held that the anomalies of this life are indisputable evidence of another. In His own eternities, he declared, God will vindicate His ways with men. "Death," he told his friends, "is just a parenthesis in life's activities. Life closes in the twilight: it opens with the dawn." Is there, in all our poetry, a lovelier line than that in which he urges us to be:—

> ... Like the bird who, pausing in her flight,
> Awhile on boughs too slight,
> Feels them give way beneath her, and yet sings
> Knowing that she hath wings.

It is difficult to think of many men who have appealed more profoundly to the heart of humanity than has he.

Creator of a Craft

When David Garrick died in 1779, three striking tributes were paid to the excellence of his character and the splendor of his influence. He was buried in Westminster Abbey with the most imposing solemnities and amidst an unprecedented concourse of mourners representative of every phase of English life; Dr. Johnson sorrowfully declared that his passing had eclipsed the gaiety of nations; and Oliver Goldsmith, in a stately ode, sang, in the most accurate, the most discriminating, and the most eloquent terms, the sterling qualities of the man whom millions lamented. By his noble life, his dazzling powers, and his masterly achievements, Garrick gave an entirely new status to the theater, and proved that an actor who takes his task seriously can become, not only a clever entertainer, but a commanding figure in the cultural life of his time.

Born in abject poverty, and willing to do anything to earn a living, he obtained employment as a scene-shifter at a small playhouse. But everybody about the place soon recognized that the boy was a born mimic. His face and voice were absolutely at the command of his will. All his powers were extraordinarily flexible. Diderot says that he once saw Garrick put his face between two screens, and, without saying a word, portray twenty different emotions in as many seconds. It was this subtle skill in the most difficult department of stagecraft that marked the young scene-shifter as an actor of the finest type and that, on his admission to the profession, secured his immediate success.

Unspoiled by Fame and Fortune

Garrick's superb personality revealed itself in the fact that, rising at a bound from obscurity to fame, from poverty to affluence, he remained delightfully unspoiled by the sensational transition. Dr. Johnson was at first very dubious about Garrick's phenomenal prosperity. It seemed to him a cruel injustice that one man should become rich by merely repeating, with grimace and gesticulations, what better men had written. But when he saw that the young actor assumed no airs, betrayed no affectations or artificialities, and clung to the friends whom he had made in his earlier days, Johnson threw his suspicions to the winds and counted the companionship of Garrick one of life's loftiest prizes.

Austin Dobson, in his assessment of Garrick's influence on history, stresses this feature as his outstanding virtue. Garrick never strutted; he was always exquisitely natural. He stood, Dobson says, for truth against tradition; for the emancipating influence of Diderot as against the retrograde influence of

Voltaire. The atmosphere of Garrick's stage technique was in perfect harmony with the atmosphere of daily life. Herein lay the basic secret of his greatness.

A Triumph of Unselfishness

To sum up the whole situation, Garrick was a great actor because he was a great man and he was a good actor because he was a good person. He moved others to deep and profound emotion because he himself felt so acutely all that he portrayed. One of his familiar cronies has told how, in a London drawing room, Garrick described an experience that had just befallen him on the street. He had seen a baker's boy mischievously salute a passing comrade. In doing so, his basket of cakes fell from his head, with the result that the buns soon littered the gutter. Garrick convulsed the entire company as he described the errand boy's earlier antics; everybody sat breathless as the actor stood dumbfounded and dismayed over the fallen basket; and, when he burst into tears over the consequent damage, there were few dry eyes in the room. And the vital truth is that the tears that the actor shed were perfectly genuine.

On the stage, as in private life, it was second nature to him to put himself in the other man's place. When he heard that his old friend Dr. Johnson was in need, he asked Albany Wallis to hand the doctor a roll of notes without revealing the source of the gift. "Wallis," exclaimed the doctor, deeply moved, "I know whence this money comes. Tell Mr. Garrick that his goodness is almost too much for me. Tell him, too, that I shall never be able to repay either this sum nor any of the amounts that he has anonymously sent me." To men of this fine type—men who owe their success to their genius for living their lives in the lives of others—the world does not grudge any laurels that eventually adorn their brows.

Father Time's Makeweight

On February 29th we have the rare satisfaction of expressing our felicitations to those unhappy people who enjoy the celebration of a birthday only once in every four years. In the shadowed careers of all such unfortunates there comes a time when they go to bed with sad thoughts on the night of February 28, and wake up with still sadder ones on the morning of March 1. They must feel like children who, after waiting for fully an hour at a railway station for the train that was to take them to the seaside, watch it rush through without stopping. They turn away cherishing a bitter disappointment. The classical case is the case of poor Frederic, the hero of *The Pirates of Penzance*—a case that is especially apposite in this particular year. It is his nurse who unfolds the pathetic story:

> When Frederic was a little lad he proved
> so brave and daring,
> His father thought he'd 'prentice him to some
> career sea-faring,

> I was, alas, his nursery-maid, and so
> it fell to my lot
>
> To take and bind the promising boy
> apprentice to a pilot.
>
> I was a stupid nursery-maid,
> on breakers always steering,
>
> And I did not catch the word aright,
> through being hard of hearing.
>
> Mistaking my instructions, which
> within my brain, did gyrate,
>
> I took and bound this promising boy
> apprentice to a pirate!

And so poor Frederic was covenanted to the pirates until his 21st birthday. On his coming-of-age, however, he broke away from his doubtful associates, moved in the most excellent society and became engaged to the beautiful Mabel Stanley. Then the trouble begins. Mabel finds Frederic in tears. What can be the matter? The matter is February 29! Frederic was born on that unhappy date, and the King of the Pirates has drawn his attention to it.

> … A terrible disclosure
>
> Has just been made to Mabel, my dearly loved
> one,
>
> I bound myself to serve the pirate captain
>
> Until I reached my one-and-twentieth birthday
>
> And I was born in Leap Year, and that birthday
>
> Will not be reached by me till 1940.

And thus, around this awkward complication, Sir W. S. Gilbert weaves all the comedy and romance of the popular opera.

Commiseration of Youth

At marriages celebrated on February 29 it is the quintessence of bad form to make the slightest allusion to the silver or the golden wedding. For February 29 comes at best, only once in four years, not always then. And since neither 25 nor 50 is divisible by four the only hope that the bride and bridegroom can cherish is the hope of celebrating the diamond wedding 60 years hence on such a scale as will atone for the omission of the silver and the golden ones. The people who are born on February 29 do get a birthday every few years, and today they will probably forget their earlier deprivations and forgive the parsimony of a capricious calendar. They will enjoy a birthday at last and will probably celebrate it on a lordly scale. Anybody who has ever been present on such an occasion must have been amused at the unmistakable undertone of commiseration that mingles with the outbursts of congratulation. A good start, it is commonly believed, is half the battle. This being so, most people feel that these February 29 victims started shockingly. On the very threshold of existence they managed matters so clumsily as to get themselves born on a day that deprives them of 75 per cent of their fair share of birthdays. To youth, this is a most egregious blunder. A child will contemplate a person born on

February 29 with eyes filled with unutterable pity and astonishment. If the ill-starred individual had been born armless or legless, the element of compassion could scarcely have been more pronounced. A birthday only once in four years! Only three birthdays in the whole course of childhood! Only about 20 in the allotted span of human existence! And fancy being unable, except in some awkward makeshift fashion, to celebrate one's coming-of-age at all. For, shuffle themselves as they may, the years can never bring the 21st birthday of a Leap Year again!

Mathematical Problem

But, on Leap Year, all such people will luxuriate in a birthday. Whether they will add one or four to their previous age is a point that must be left to their own honor and to their sense of the fitness of things. Miss Priscilla Pettigrew was born, it will be remembered, on February 29, and she held strongly that it would seem like cheating to add more than one to her age in virtue of a single birthday. "I'd be downright ashamed," she indignantly protested, "to add four to myself every time a birthday happened to come round! I couldn't bear to make honest folks believe I was that much older than I really am!" A conscience so sensitive and so scrupulous, presents us with a most affecting and most edifying moral spectacle, but it cannot be commended without reserve as a model for general emulation. Let the young people who, today, indulge in birthday festivities, be in no hurry to adopt Miss Pettigrew's method of computation! If, flushed with the excitement of the rare occasion, they feel attracted to the scheme, it will be necessary for their grave and reverend seniors, who never fail to recognize in a birthday an opportunity of administering liberal potations of good advice, to do their duty. These venerable wiseacres must, out of the hoarded wealth of their long experience, inform the happy birthday celebrants that a singular and tragic Nemesis has invariably overtaken those who have modeled their behavior on that of the amiable and conscientious Priscilla. They have, it is true, added only one to their age on the arrival of each quadrennial birthday, but, on the other hand, it has been noticed that, in every case, they have died remarkably young. Miss Pettigrew herself was no exception. The bloom of her virgin beauty began to fade before she was 10. By the time she was 15 there was a perceptible stoop in her shoulders and the silver was rapidly creeping into her hair. With her 18th birthday still 18 months ahead of her, she went down to her grave looking strangely bent and wrinkled and old!

Eccentric Calendar

Perhaps we have been a trifle slipshod in referring to the birthdays of Twenty-Ninth-February children as being quadrennial. They are scarcely that. For Leap Year is an occasional, rather than a regular, visitor. Babies who are born on that awkward date cannot rely upon a birthday even once in four years. In his essay on "The New Year's Coming of Age," Charles Lamb describes the famous feast to which all the days had been invited. The greatest care had been taken properly to place the guests. The special days, the fast days, the festival days were all given seats at table that were deemed suitable to the honor usually paid them. The most baffling of all the invited guests was the Twenty-Ninth-of-February. His erratic appearances seemed to perplex everybody and nobody could be certain whether he intended being present or not. And yet, if the other days would only take the trouble to understand him, there is method in his seeming madness. He arrives in the course of every fourth year except at the end of a century, and then he only comes when the first two figures of the year's name are divisible by four. Thus the years 1700, 1800, and 1900 were not Leap Years while the year 1600 was and the year 2000 will be. Miss Priscilla Pettigrew was born, as everybody knows, on February 29, 1764. She celebrated her eighth birthday in 1796, but she had to wait until 1804 for her ninth! Those who were born on February 29 any time during the Nineteenth Century and who lived to the dawn of the Twentieth, suffered a similar deprivation when the year 1901 broke upon them. But those who come into the world this February 29, or on any February 29 this century, are safe. For the year 2000 will behave handsomely by them. If they wish to go eight years without a birthday they must contrive, by hook or by crook, to live until the year 2100 comes round.

Splinters of Time

The fact is that February 29 is a piece of chronological padding. It is a matter of makeweight. The earth takes 365 days 5 hours 48 minutes 46 seconds to complete its circuit round the sun, and our Leap Year arrangement is the best contrivance yet invented for tucking the odd hours into the calendar. The ancients got over the difficulty by dividing the year into 12 months of 30 days each, and every now and again—whenever they found the seasons getting out of order—they took a holiday, giving the days neither numbers nor names, until they got the whole thing into shape once more. How the babies born in those unrecognized intervals managed their birthdays we are not told. Perhaps they never had any, in which case a modern Twenty-Ninth-Of-February child is, by comparison, in clover.

Laureate of the West

The poet, Henry Longfellow, was born on February 27, 1807. For his own sake, as well as for the sake of the work that he did, he richly deserves to be remembered. As a boy he conceived a lofty ideal, and, throughout a long career, he never for a moment swerved from it. His father wanted him to be a lawyer. Henry begged to be excused. "I most eagerly aspire," he told his parents at the age of seventeen, "to eminence in literature; my whole soul burns most ardently for it, my every thought centers there. Surely there never was a better opportunity offered for the exertion of literary talent than is offered now!" America was in the making; a new world was taking shape; the hour seemed sublime.

He was fortunate in being appointed, while still in his teens, to a professorship of modern languages at Bowdoin College. Holding such a position, he was able to devote himself to literature with the necessary detachment and without the torment of anxiety that many young authors are forced to endure. He wrote carefully, travelled widely, and became not only one of the most popular poets, but one of the most commanding personalities of his time. His very appearance favored him. Kingsley declared that Longfellow's was the most beautiful face that he had ever seen. Broad shouldered and of well-knit frame with finely-cut features, eloquent eyes and a voice that was singularly deep, flexible, melodious, and full of tenderness, his personality was richly and attractively equipped. Nor did this pleasing exterior convey an exaggerated impression of the superb quality of the man. "He was," says Thomas Davidson, "as nearly perfect as it is possible for human nature to be. He united in his strong, transparent humanity almost every virtue under heaven. No man ever lived more completely in the light than he." The choicest spirits of Europe and America were proud of being numbered among his friends.

The Chequered Evolution of a Classic

The greatest day in Longfellow's life was that on which, he published *Evangeline*. He was forty at the time. And the singular thing is that, in seizing upon this graceful story and weaving it into a romance, he was simply rescuing from oblivion what others had contemptuously, tossed to the rubbish heap. It happened that Nathaniel Hawthorne, Longfellow's school-fellow and life-long companion, came one day to dine with the poet at Craigie House, bringing with him a friend, a clergyman. The cleric, who had been delving among the records of the Nova Scotia rebellion, told the story of the frustrated wedding of two young people at Grand Pre; of their cruel separation by force of arms; of Evangeline's long, long quest; and of their reunion on the day of Gabriel's death. Turning to Hawthorne, he suggested that the record would furnish excellent material for the plot of a novel.

Oddly enough, Hawthorne sniffed at it. He was afflicted with what psychologists would call a miasmatic conscience. He could make nothing of a story into which no sinister element entered; he liked a villain as a foil for the splendors of his hero; he could see no possibilities in the pretty but unexciting story of a woman's endless search for her lost lover. "Well then," said Longfellow, "if you really do not want this story for a novel, let me have it for a poem!" And so it was agreed. As Longfellow perused the tragic annals of the period in which the plot is laid, he was impressed by the magnificence of the opportunity that Hawthorne had so peremptorily discarded; he chivalrously wrote to his friend urging him to reconsider his disdainful decision; but Hawthorne had made up his mind and declined to reopen the question. Thereupon Longfellow applied himself seriously to the enticing task. He did his work so well that Hawthorne himself, falling in love with the poem, read it so often that he almost knew it by heart, and, when dying he had it read aloud to him by a friend beside his bed.

The Art of Setting History to Music

Longfellow had an amazing genius for crystallizing into tuneful poesy the inner sentiment of history. In *Evangeline*, in *Hiawatha*, and in *The Courtship of Miles Standish*, he was dealing with facts. His art lay in setting those facts to music without doing the slightest violence to the actual truth. He brought a certain amount of imagination to the Evangeline story; he suffused it with a strong and sublimated emotion; yet the reader instinctively feels that the tale as Longfellow tells it is probably a more faithful portrayal of the circumstances than a bald and lifeless record would have been. *Hiawatha* appeared seven years later. "I have hit upon a plan," he writes, excitedly, "for a poem on the Red Indians. It seems to me the right plan and the only one. It is to weave their beautiful traditions into a concerted whole. I have hit upon a measure, too, which exactly suits the theme." And now that, as the fruit of this inspiration, we have *Hiawatha*, are we to regard it as pure poetry, concrete history or a medley of both?

Bancroft, the historian, congratulated Longfellow on the fidelity of the poem to Indian life and Indian tradition. In *The Courtship of Miles Standish*, the poet is again absolutely loyal to the spirit of the historic narrative, even if he sometimes brings his fancy to bear upon the letter of it. And, after all, as Sir Walter Scott has proved, it is the spirit of the storied past rather than the letter that constitutes true history. Longfellow's most glaring defect lay in his excessive modesty. His brilliant academic gifts would have enabled him to strike a note as profound and as sublime as anything that Tennyson has given us. But he aspired to nothing so pretentious. Yet, contenting himself with singing a few dainty and deathless songs, he contrived, as W. D. Howells has pointed out, to secure standing and recognition for the literature of America among the classical treasures of the older world.

Pastels of Sound

As summer fades imperceptivity into autumn, nature abounds in an infinite variety of soft tints and quiet colors. Moreover, the ear has its pastel shades as well as the eye. The symphony of life is very largely molded on its undertones—the whispering among the leaves, the humming of insects, the sigh of the breeze, the twittering of birds, the lapping of waves, and all those gentle and subdued sounds that, every day of our lives, soothe and strengthen us. On the very last page of his *Confessions of an Uncommon Attorney*, Reginald Hine paints a picture of the idyllic scenes amidst which he is laying aside his pen. It is a beautiful estate at Minsden, in Hertfordshire, the haunt of every kind of wild flower and of every species of feathered songster. The picturesque ruins of a fourteenth century church add to its charm. It would, Mr. Hine says, be a lovely place to die in.

Peaceful as it is, however, he makes it clear that its tranquillity does not consist in its silence, "The very air," he says, "is tremulous with that faint murmur— call it the undersong of earth, the music of the spheres, the sight of departed time, or what you will—which only the more attuned spirits overhear:—

> Stillness accompanied with sound so soft
> Charms more than silence. Meditation here
> May think down hours to moments.

"For those who have ears to hear," Mr. Hine concludes, "how peaceful and assuaging it is to listen to the zephyr's call, the night wind's lovely vesper hymn!" These are the pastel sounds that sweeten and sanctify earth's silences.

Softer than Silence More Eloquent than Speech

For silence in itself can be maddening. As those who have endured solitary confinement know, silence hath its horrors no less renowned than noise. What was the world like before the hurricane of mechanization awoke the screech and the crash and the roar by which all modern generations have been tortured? In a state of nature, Man would be familiar with many sounds; but it is safe to assume that they would all be beneficent sounds—pleasant sounds designed for his delectation and unpleasant sounds designed to warn him of the proximity of his natural enemies. Between a sound and a noise there is all the difference in the world. A noise will awaken a child; the mother, in restoring it to its slumbers, will resort, not to silence, but to sound; she will croon a lullaby.

A recent traveler tells how he arrived one evening, very tired, at an English seaside resort. Obtaining a room at a hotel, he retired early, but not to sleep. Holiday-makers chattered, giggled, and exchanged raucous inanities in the corridor; and, just as things promised to simmer down, a theater round the corner began to disgorge its patrons, unleashing a babel of tootings, changings of gear and all the confusion incidental to congested motor traffic. But, at long last, he says, there came, not silence, but something infinitely sweet and soothing—the distant sound of the waves upon the shore, the murmur and the music of the sea.

The incident reminds us of Lockhart's beautiful description of the passing of Sir Walter Scott. It was not by silence, but by something lovelier, that his last moments were solaced. "It was so quiet a day that the sound he loved best, the gentle ripple of the Tweed over its pebbles, was distinctly audible as we knelt around his bed while his eldest son kissed and closed his eyes." Sir Walter's requiem was chanted by Nature in her choicest pastel tones.

Nature's Accompaniment to Humanity's Passion

In one of his greatest novels, Trollope declares that there is scarcely a mood that such sounds will not match. Resting near the Rhine, his heroine is enjoying the delicious music of its rapidly moving waters. "If you are chatting with your friend," Trollope observes, "such melodious sounds wrap up your speech, keeping it to your two selves. If you would sleep, it is of all lullabies the sweetest. If you are alone, and would think, it aids your thoughts. If you are alone, and, because thought would be too painful, you do not wish to think, it gently dispels your sorrow." All this goes to show that, while silence is infinitely preferable to noise, there is something even more grateful to the ear than silence. Such subdued sounds mingle with the songs of life and with the silences of life to produce that essential symphony of repose in which the ordinary man may find his soul. Every man should, occasionally, lend his ear to the undertones of life. "Give me my scallop shell of quiet!" begged Sir Walter Raleigh in the poem that he penned just before his execution; and, in making that eloquent request, he speaks for us all.

All through life the voices that most profoundly impress us, and that most imperatively command us, are gentle and perfectly controlled voices. We may be hectored into compliance by bellow and bluster, but it is the whisper that more often secures our wholehearted cooperation.

Is it any wonder then, that the Divine voice, whenever and wherever heard, is invariably marked by softness, calmness, and restraint? The most convincing and compelling exhibitions of superhuman power come to men, not in the earthquake nor in the fire, but in the still small voice. Reason speaks in an undertone; so does conscience; and so does revelation. In one of his most rapturous and seraphic predictions concerning the coming Redeemer, the prophet Isaiah declares that His voice shall be quiet, subdued, restrained. "He shall not scream nor shout, nor advertise Himself." His utterance, that is to say, shall be expressive, persuasive, effective; but there shall be nothing loud or self-assertive about it. The eloquence of heaven is always couched in pastel accents and in delicate and melodious undertones.

Rhetoric in Stone

Few men have been so famous as was Sir Christopher Wren; no man has been as famous for so long. We associate him only with the erection of St. Paul's Cathedral; but 30 years before the Great Fire which necessitated the creation of that stately fane, Isaac Barrow said of him: "As a boy, Christopher Wren was a prodigy; as a man, he is a miracle; indeed, he is a superman." Wren was then 30.

"I must affirm," wrote Robert Hooke, the renowned mathematician, "that, since the time of Archimedes, there never met in one man so mechanical a hand and so philosophical a mind." Is there, in the entire realm of universal, another instance of a youth earning such testimonies from men of such a caliber before his real life work had properly begun?

Among all the arts and crafts, the sciences and industries of life, there is scarcely one that his youthful mind did not invade with a view to improving existing conditions. He takes a stroll into the country; sees a farmer laboriously sowing his corn; and straightway invents a contrivance which will do the work in a tenth of the time. He hears a sailor telling of his sufferings at sea for lack of water, and at once brings into being a condensing machine. He gathers about him a cluster of kindred spirits, and thus the Royal Society springs into existence.

Being at once a skillful astronomer and a master mechanic, he treated matters celestial and matters terrestrial with equal facility and familiarity. Devoting himself to the study of medicine, he invented a method of blood transfusion and busied himself with an apparatus for purifying and fumigating sick rooms. There was nothing in the world or out of it that he deemed beyond the range of his investigation. His insatiable curiosity penetrated every crack and crevice in the universe. Nothing eluded him. He is the outstanding example of a man who, Jack of all trades, is master of every one.

A City's Extremity: an Architect's Opportunity

If he anticipated fame, he certainly did not anticipate it as the designer of a great cathedral. He was immersed in his researches in his laboratory and his surgery when, in 1666, his sublime opportunity burst dramatically upon him. London was a sea of flame. The fire was extinguished on September 8, and, four days later, Wren, then 34, sought an audience of the King and laid before him a comprehensive plan for rebuilding the metropolis.

The performance stands as one of the most bewildering triumphs of creative art; and nobody has quite forgiven the short-sighted authorities of that stagnant period for rejecting a scheme so swiftly and brilliantly conceived. Parts of the plan, including the designs for the erection of St. Paul's Cathedral, and of about 50 other churches, were accepted; and the beauty of those completed parts tantalizes the imagination by fleeting visions of what might have been.

St. Paul's—Wren's masterpiece—took 35 years in building. With what pathetic pride and tenderness the old architect watched it grow! Amid the decay of his physical and intellectual powers, he insisted on being carried down to the city every now and again that, with his fast-dimming eyes, he might actually see the fulfilment of his splendid dream. Happily, he lived to see it finished. He was nearly 80.

Thirteen years later, the noble fane extended to him the hospitality of sepulchre. Over the doorway, close to his tomb, the visitor ponders the historic inscription: "If thou seekest his monument, look around!" As long as London stands, and as long as English history is read with patriotic pride, his will be one of the names that will always be cherished with reverent gratitude. Neither three centuries nor thirty will obliterate his memory from the hearts of his admiring countrymen.

Ministry and Minstrelsy of Granite

Thanks to Sir Christopher Wren, the stones of St. Paul's speak with an eloquence peculiarly their own. There are things that can be said in granite and marble that can be said as forcefully in no other way. In his essay on "The Study of Architecture," Mr. H. H. Bishop points out that even the loveliness and majesty of Nature would stand denuded and impoverished if such buildings as St. Paul's Cathedral were allowed to fall, into decay.

He mentions a dozen cities that would instantly descend from grandeur to mediocrity if the architectural triumphs that distinguish them were suddenly removed. And the reason is, Mr. Bishop maintains, that architecture speaks; destroy it, and the silence becomes oppressive. "Egyptian architecture," he insists, "conveyed to all nations the idea of eternity; the Grecian, beauty; the Roman, power; the Gothic, faith; and so on." That being so, what impression does St. Paul's make?

Mr. Bishop maintains that the stones of St. Paul's combine, in exquisite harmony the voices that are heard in the noblest erections of antiquity. He who visits St. Paul's feels himself to be the heir of all the glories of his country's history and of his Redeemer's faith. He is on the holiest of holy grounds. Every stone has a voice, and every voice is an ascription, a litany, a prayer. When, in the form of St. Paul's, Sir Christopher Wren gave visible expression to the vision that, in the silences, he had beheld, he poured from his enraptured soul a cloistral and deathless poem.

So long as the cathedral stands on its stately hill, surmounted by its "cross of gold that shines over city and river," it will remind every man within sight of its commanding dome of things too holy to be adequately said or sung. Wren was determined that all men, in city or suburb, in turning their eyes towards the gleaming cross that he lifted skywards, should salute in it, not only the center of London, but the center of everything besides.

The Lamps of Liberty

In the days immediately preceding the Great Plague and the Great Fire, two men pored over manuscripts that were destined to mold the ages. John Milton was busy with his *Paradise Lost*; Baruch Spinoza, a man of 30, whose eyes glistened with the tell-tale luster that betokens the ravages of consumption, was putting the finishing touches to his *Ethics*.

He was born on November 24, 1632 at Amsterdam. The boyhood of Spinoza was spent in a Jewish home of the best type. The sacred traditions of the Synagogue were in his blood. His grandfather and his father had been revered and honored leaders in Israel. The fact that he was named Baruch, the Blessed, while his sisters were Rebekah and Miriam, indicates the atmosphere in which the philosopher was reared.

Epic of Intellectual Independence

The most momentous event of his youth was his determination to learn Latin. Three essential developments attended this step. The first was that he selected as his tutor a doctor named Van Den Ende, an extraordinary character, who was hanged in Paris in 1674. The second was that he fell in love with his teacher's pretty daughter, who, a little later, jilted him. And the third was that his new acquirement brought him into touch with modern philosophy and opened up a new world. As a result of this adventure he felt himself to be moving on another plane and speaking another language. His old associates suspected his orthodoxy, and, in point of fact, he himself was not very sure of it. He was offered a thousand florins a year to reaffirm his attachment to his old faith. He indignantly refused, and, in 1656 was solemnly excommunicated from the Commonwealth of Israel.

His behavior at this crisis was characteristic of him. His mind was on pilgrimage and must be free to follow its own bent. Later on, although poorer than any church mouse, he declined a pension from the French king, and an appointment as Professor of Philosophy at the University of Heidelberg, lest acceptance of such tempting boons should commit him to teach a little more or a little less than, at the moment, he really believed. Than Spinoza, the world has never known a more honest man.

Robbed of Fame by Early Death

In the course of his brief career, his disciples, pitying his physical frailty, made him handsome gifts, but, for the most part, he supported himself by laboring with his own hands. Like all young Jews of the period, he had learned a trade. He was a skillful polisher of lenses; and the spectacles, microscopes, and telescopes that proceeded from his bench were held in the highest repute. Unfortunately, however, the dust resulting from the constant grinding and filing of glasses irritated his crazy lungs, aggravating his malady, and hastening his death.

One of his greatest admirers was Henry Oldenburg, the first secretary of the Royal Society. Oldenburg more than once visited the little cottage in which Spinoza boarded, and through the years maintained with him a voluminous correspondence. As time went on, however, Oldenburg began to find himself out of his depth. He twitted his old friend with having forsaken philosophy for theology; he was spending too much of his time with angels and archangels.

The simple fact was that, the more Spinoza probed the mysteries of matter and mind, the more certain he became of that spiritual realm in which these things live and move and have their being. Like Milton, his illustrious contemporary, he felt that earth is but the shadow of heaven. He talked more and more about God as the source of all things, the home of all things, and the destiny of all things. He came to love God and was eager that all men should know and love Him, too. In a phrase that has stuck to his name, Novalis called him the God-intoxicated man.

Milton made his way through the charred ruins of the metropolis to sell his ponderous manuscript for five pounds to a very nervous publisher. Spinoza was robbed of even that meager satisfaction. His consumption slew him at 44. He left just enough goods and chattels to pay his debts and funeral expenses. His greatest work, published long after his death, was hailed by the most eminent critics as a masterpiece; and, although now superseded or incorporated in the works of later writers, it exercised a profound influence on the thinkers of the 18th and 19th centuries.

A Cheer for the Year

New Year's day marks both a burial and a birth. We stand reverently by the graveside of the past; we gaze curiously into the cradle of the year just born. It is at such moments that we exhibit, in full-orbed perfection, life's two monumental chivalries. A natural instinct restrains us from speaking ill of the dead; we are in honor bound to think as kindly as we can of the year that has passed, forgiving its blemishes and magnifying its benefits. And, as to the year that sprawls in its infancy before us, it becomes us to treat it as we ourselves were treated in similar circumstances.

Is there anything in the solar system more beautiful than the faith which on our first arrival, our parents reposed in us? They knew that we should be human, yet they idealized us until they thought of us as almost divine. They dreamed of all the good things we should do, and never for a moment suspected the bad. In their enraptured eyes, an aureole already encircled our brows. It is with some such rainbow-tinted chivalry that we extend our welcome to a newborn year.

Few things are more intriguing than our capacity for scraping together a presentable stock of glittering optimism at this particular season. We are subtly conscious of having turned a corner; entered upon a fresh phase, rounded a cape into warmer latitudes and sunnier seas. Something tells us that however unkind our yesterdays may have been, our tomorrows are unanimously and whole-heartedly on the side of the angels.

The High Art of Self-Culture

In a sense, such mental processes and reactions are wholly illogical, perhaps a trifle absurd. After all, the year is a cycle. Nature recognizes no day as its beginning; she indignantly scorns the thought of a close. To her, the succession of the seasons represents the inspired mechanism of perpetual motion. She knows no weariness, no monotony, no senility, no end. In spite of this, however, there is a modicum of sound sense in marking a certain point in the beginningless and endless circle, and in making that mystic point the theater of a little discreet heart-searching. Are we on the right track? What progress are we making? Are we appreciably nearer our goal than when we last took our bearings?

Obviously, the highest attainment in life consists in making the best of ourselves. But it is not easy. The outstanding fact in each man's pilgrimage is the terrifying fact of his own individuality. Each man is a pathfinder, blazing a trail through an unexplored continent. There are no maps or charts. Nobody else has ever had his life to live. Nobody else's experience, therefore, can serve him as a guide book for his own lonely trudge. By hook or by crook, he must find his way as he struggles on.

Wisdom of Taking One's Bearings

It is all very well for metaphysicians and theorists to write books on *Life and How to Live It*; such a treatise is useless to the average man. He abhors the general; he craves the particular. He wants a book dealing distinctively with his own personal life. It must begin with his own birth; it must reach its climax with his own death; it must have his photograph as its frontispiece. And, because nobody on earth is competent to write it, and because nobody but himself would wish to read it, such a volume has never been published, and, in the nature of things, never will be.

It follows that if a man is to develop his personality and fulfill his mission in life at all successfully, he must stand occasionally on some lofty eminence, from the commanding heights of which he can survey the country that he has already traversed and map out for himself a path through the unknown territory that melts into infinity before him. Herein lies the rationale of our New Year celebrations. We arbitrarily fix a point in the circle as the beginning and the end of that circle; and on reaching that mysterious point, we pause to readjust ourselves to ourselves, to one another, to those around us, to God above us, and to the eternal scheme of things.

A Literary Calamity

I t is good to remember the day when, John Stuart Mill
drove up to the home of the Carlyles in Cheyne Row
to make an astounding confession. When Carlyle had
completed the first volume of his *French Revolution*, he
lent the manuscript to Mill for inspection and suggestion.
In some way, that has never been satisfactorily explained,
Mill left it in such a position that his housemaid mistook
it for waste paper, and burned it! It is to the everlasting
honor of Carlyle that, although the revelation almost
broke his heart, he never let Mill realize the immensity
of his deprivation. Carlyle is one of the truly Homeric
figures of our literary history. The interest that we feel
in him is the interest that we feel in Vesuvius. Other
great men are like great mountains; they leap from
the common plane and stand out with grandeur
and ruggedness against the horizon; but Carlyle is
essentially volcanic. His personality is awe-inspiring;
his temperament is fiery; his utterance is like a turgid
flow of lava. He holds for us the fascination that attaches
to all things that are terrible, weird, explosive. He takes
knowing. The reader who picks up *Sartor Resartus* or

The French Revolution for the first time feels that he is crossing a ploughed field in silk slippers. The going is hard and the gait ungraceful; but there is novelty in it, and after a while he gets accustomed to the rough track and begins to enjoy the smell of the upturned soil and the tang of the bracing air. Feeling a personal interest in this strange and uncouth writer, he proceeds to the biographies. Little by little he gets to know Carlyle, and for some time at any rate does not altogether like him. He contemplates the writer's personality much as a small boy contemplates a caged bear. He is glad to have seen something of him, but he does not sigh for a closer acquaintance. The great man is all snaps and snarls and grunts and growls. We are repelled by his tactlessness towards his wife, by his ill-temper towards the unfortunates who incur his displeasure, and by his constant approximation to savagery. Yet, just as, in the one case, the boy will gladly walk a good many miles to see the bear again, so in the other, we only need a fresh invitation to study Carlyle, and we cheerfully respond. The geologists have taught us that the world is all the better and all the safer for having a few volcanoes and it is certainly the better for having men of the type of Thomas Carlyle.

Carlyle stands, and stands conspicuously, among the prophets of the ages. He was, as Edmund Scherer, the French scholar, declares, the prophet of sincerity. Truth was his passion; he was tremendously in earnest. "Mr. Carlyle is no homoeopathist," said Mazzini, his Italian contemporary; "he never administers remedies for evil in infinitesimal doses; he never pollutes the sacredness of thought by outward concession or compromise with error. Like Luther, he hurls his inkstand at the devil without looking to the consequences; but he does it with such transparent sincerity that the devil himself could not be displeased as it were the moment not critical, and every blow of the inkstand a serious thing to him." There, then, stands the prophet—the prophet of sincerity—as great in his way as any prophet of the olden time! "No prophet," says Dr. Maclean Watt, "ever gripped and shook his generation with such a horny hand and such a grasp invincible." Dr. Watt contrasts Carlyle with Ruskin. "Ruskin approaches all his themes as if in broadcloth and with his gloves on; but the rugged Scotsman walks out with his budget of kingly truths, and, no matter what clothing he wears, you feel the homespun and naked grip of a strong man's influence." When Carlyle was an old man of 80, Lord Beaconsfield, in the Queen's name, offered him a peerage and an income capable of maintaining its rank and dignity. Such a distinction had never before been offered to any man of letters, and Carlyle was not unmindful of the honor done him. But he shook his shaggy old head. A prophet with a peerage and a lordly pension! "Very proper of the Queen to offer it," observed a London bus-conductor to J. A. Froude next day; "very proper of her to offer it, and more proper of he to say that he would have nothing to do with it." "'Tisn't the likes of they who can do honor to the likes of he!" Froude agreed with the conductor. "Yet," he adds, "the country was saved by the offer from the reproach of coming centuries, when Carlyle will stand among his contemporaries as Socrates stands among the Athenians, the one pre-eminently wise man to whom the rest are nothing." Thomas Carlyle as a peer of the realm would have cut an odd figure in polite society, yet we all like to think that he was excluded from that charmed circle; not by the ostracism of aristocracy, but by his own deliberate choice.

The lure of Carlyle arises in part from our invincible love of fair play. We instinctively feel that, at least in his early days, Carlyle received something less than justice. For years he lived in poverty among the moss-hags of Craigenputtock, writing the books that have taken their place among the immortals. But in those dour days, nobody recognized their worth. The honest man had put all his soul into what he had written; he would not modify a single sentence in order to render his work more acceptable to the popular palate. He had expressed himself in his own rugged way; he was too sure of himself to smooth out his style in order to harmonize it with the recognized standards. And then, with the proud consciousness of a good and honest workman, he resolved to test the market. He hoped to receive £200 for his manuscript; the publishers offered to print it if he paid them £150! A friend advised him to wait. "I will—to the end of eternity rather!" Carlyle replied. And he waited seven years, writing all the time. And when at length *Sartor Resartus* saw the light of day its reception was anything but sympathetic. One of the most influential critics of the period described it as a heap of nonsense. Through many years the judgment of those who occupy seats of authority was doubtful, if not actually hostile. A writer in *Blackwood's* declared bluntly that Carlyle was a blatant impostor. The London *World* assured its readers that "there is little that is extraordinary, still less that is heroic, in the character of Thomas Carlyle. Full of littleness and weakness of shallow dogmatism and blustering conceit, he must soon be forgotten—the sooner the better." Such opinions as these continued to be expressed to the end of his life, and even his biographers damned him with faint praise. It was said of Froude that he took his master's body from the grave with a pitch fork and turned it round and round to show his fellowmen, what very common clay it was.

The minds of men have revolted against this kind of thing. The world is equally shocked by fulsome eulogy and by unmerited severity. Recognizing that Carlyle received less than was his due, men delight in reviewing his work and making tardy acknowledgment of his greatness. When he died, a grave in Westminster Abbey was offered, and like the peerage and the pension, declined. He had begged that he might be buried beside his father and mother in the old church yard at Ecclefechan by the Solway. For, beneath a stern and forbidding exterior, there dwelt in Carlyle a deep, rich, vein of human tenderness. It was his genuine love for his fellow-men that inspired his faith in the justice of posterity. When his contemporaries treated him with scorn, he waved his hand to the unborn generations. With all his surliness, his querulousness, his impatience and his ill-temper, he remains as Lord Morley said, one of the mightiest moral forces of all time, and his influence upon our literature is as wholesome as it is permanent.

A Study in Light and Shade

Beyond the shadow of a doubt, Edmund Burke, is one of the most magnetic, one of the most baffling and one of the most indefinable personalities in our history. On what does his reputation rest? Two questions immediately present themselves. Was Burke a great statesman? Was he a great orator? If he was a great statesman, to what party did he belong? And why, in an age that often lacked vigorous leadership, did he never become Prime Minister? Again, if he was a great orator, why was he repeatedly coughed down or left to address benches from which practically all the members had fled? Nobody would seriously claim that Burke was a front-ranked statesman. He possessed none of those outstanding gifts that enable dominating figures to mold parties to their will and lead them with autocratic authority. And, as to his rhetoric, it was a thing of fits and starts. He often soared, but, just as often, he groveled. Occasionally dazzling in his brilliance, he was just as often unconscionably dull. He would talk pompously and interminably on insignificant themes and fail lamentably to seize the opportunity presented by really noble occasions.

Of all his weaknesses, his most unpardonable frailty was his inordinate fondness for dramatic display. He strained after effect. It is one of the inviolable traditions of the House of Commons to scowl on anything of the kind. The average member hates fireworks. Burke was too much of an actor for the staid and somber environment in which he found himself. He played to the gallery and there was no gallery to applaud. But this, of course, is not the whole story. Burke had other moments, inspired moments, when, as Bancroft puts it, the glowing words showered from him like burning oracles. At such times, Green says, his oratory was remarkable for its passionate ardor, its poetic fancy, its amazing prodigality of resources and for the bewildering succession in which irony, pathos, invective, humor, tenderness, vivid description, and cogent reasoning followed one another.

The Fine Frenzy Born of Inspiration

At his best, Burke was dynamic, overwhelming, irresistible. While his dramatic gift sometimes betrayed him into excesses, there were occasions when he could use it with electrical effect. During an electioneering speech at Bristol he was handed a note saying that his opponent had suddenly died. Burke paused, contemplated the missive amidst intense silence, communicated its contents to the vast audience and then tossing the document on to the table exclaimed: "Such shadows we are and such shadows we pursue!"

Dr. Johnson attributed Burke's power to a certain fineness of texture in the composition of his mind, a quality that needed some galvanic stimulus to awaken it. The astounding thing about the utterances that were delivered under such conditions is that the finest passages in those stately flights were composed on the spur of the moment. When he produced speeches to which he had devoted long and laborious study, he was usually stilted, unnatural and ineffective; but when, roused to sudden anger or enthusiasm, he sprang to his feet and poured forth the pent-up passion of his soul, he swept everything before him.

Many of his more sublime utterances have passed into classical literature. The language appears majestic; each phrase is a gleaming and exquisite pearl. Not once, nor twice, but again and again he astonished even his most ardent admirers by prodigies of intellectual audacity and achievement. His power of projection was not merely startling; it was positively uncanny. At the moment at which Capt. Arthur Phillip was stepping ashore at Sydney Cove in 1788 to inaugurate the spacious drama of Australian history, Burke was absorbed in the preparation of his impeachment of Warren Hastings. That speech stands, not only as his masterpiece, but as one of the marvels of universal literature.

Imaginative Splendor Becomes Articulate

Burke had never seen India; yet he spoke for hours as if he had spent the whole of his life among fakirs, nabobs, and rajahs. It seemed incredible that one who could speak with such picturesque realism had never actually witnessed the scenes that he so vividly and tellingly described. The bazaars, the jungles, the rice fields, and the palm groves of the East have seldom been painted more gorgeously or more convincingly than Burke painted them in the course of those brilliant flights of passionate and panoramic oratory with which he held spellbound, hour after hour, the princes, peers and parliamentarians assembled amidst the solemn grandeur of Westminster Hall. Such powers were almost superhuman.

Moreover, his most caustic critics had to admit that his character matched his powers, for Edmund Burke was the soul of goodness. When, for example, George Crabbe, totally unknown, was starving in London, conscious of the gift of poesy yet unable to secure the publication of a single stanza, he wrote in sheer desperation to Burke, then at the zenith of his career. Although Burke had never so much as heard Crabbe's name, he was impressed by the elegance and dignity of the letter, and in the most sympathetic and generous terms, immediately responded, giving his suppliant money, advice, and an introduction to wealthy and influential friends. And most amazing and most creditable of all, Burke took the poverty-stricken young poet into his own home and cared for him until he was well on his way to success. As generation succeeds generation, the world will increasingly admire the mental vigor that enabled this impulsive Irish youth, who had enjoyed few advantages, to perform such masterly feats of scholarship and eloquence. He has taken his place in history as a man who, consistently losing sight of his own interests in promoting those of his country, has left a stainless record of which the world will always be proud.

An Explosive Genius

A n hour with Walter Savage Landor is like a visit to the zoo. It is highly entertaining and instructive, but you come away with a vivid memory of gleaming fangs and ominous growls. Living to be nearly 90, he spent most of his time in singing like an archangel and fuming like a fiend. It is difficult to discover the name of one individual among his kinsfolk and acquaintances with whom, at some time, if not at all times, he did not violently quarrel. He looked superbly leonine. His head was said to have been the most magnificent that Italian painters and sculptors had ever seen, but when they begged him to sit for them he shook his glorious locks impatiently and, with a sniff of fine disdain, pursued his royal way. His second name was prophetically inspired, for with great kindness of heart he mingled barbaric ferocity and an abominable temper.

Among the authentic records is the story of a certain day on which, as he sat at table, he noticed that the joint had been ruined in the kitchen. Waxing furious, he sent for the cook and threw open the window. On the arrival of the culprit, to the amazement of the household, he hurled from the casement, not the ill-prepared sirloin but the terrified offender. He afterwards expressed sorrow, not at having hazarded the limbs and the life of the unhappy cook, but at having made a frightful mess of the seedlings in the flower beds! Yet some of the most masterly English ever given to the world bears his name. He was a born artist. The craftsmanship of letters was to him an almost sacred thing. From his earliest boyhood he cherished an exalted ideal as to how a sentence should be turned. No painter ever approached his easel animated by a purer zest for the expression of beauty on canvas than Landor felt when he set himself to the construction of a paragraph or a poem.

Content with Nothing Short of Perfection

Not only had he something to say—a generous flow of intellectual inspiration—but he was determined to make the articulation of his soul as accurate and as tuneful as the limitations of language would permit. To use one word more than was absolutely necessary would have been to him the unpardonable sin but it was of even greater importance that each word selected should be the most impressive and the most sweet-sounding and the best language was to him what melody is to the composer, what color is to the painter. Any misuse or abuse of it would be a kind of sacrilege. And the extraordinary thing is that, conceiving these exalted ideas as a schoolboy, he held true to them through a literary career that lasted for nearly 70 years. From the penning of his first poems in 1794 until he laid aside his pen in 1863, he did not once waver in his clear vision of what English prose and English poetry should be.

As soon as he set to work—and he was only 20 when his first work was published—it became clear that a genius of the purest and most dazzling type had appeared on the horizon of English letters. Southey, going into transports of delight over Landor's earliest ventures, eagerly sought his friendship, while in the year in which Nelson perished so gloriously at Trafalgar the boy Shelley used to march up and down the playgrounds of Eton declaiming the stately periods of Landor at the top of his voice. To such minds Landor's work made a resistless appeal. Charles Lamb, William Hazlitt, Thomas de Quincey, and, at a later date, Charles Dickens, Ralph Waldo Emerson, and Thomas Carlyle all fell under the wand of the magician. Each in turn saluted Landor as an oracle. The pity of it is that his vogue was almost exclusively confined to such master minds. Sidney Colvin opens his monograph on Landor by declaring that few men have ever impressed their peers so much, or the general public so little, as did he. It is a striking claim and a striking confession, revealing both the triumph and the tragedy of Landor.

Victimized by Variegated Enthusiasms

Like most fiery and impulsive natures, Landor was a man of overwhelming enthusiasms, and the wonder is not that he outgrew some of them but that he remained loyal to so many of them for so long. As a boy in his teens he was swept off his feet by a pretty Irish girl, Sophia Jane Swift, afterwards the Countess de Molande. It was purely a boy and girl infatuation, and neither of them took it seriously. She was known as Jane Landor, and he with poetic magic, transformed this into Ianthe. As Ianthe he embalmed her beauty in his poems. And though their lives were lived apart, and though he was nearly 80 when he heard of her death, he penned another poem in which he celebrated his delight that not all the oceans of the world could wash out his numerous tributes to her girlish loveliness. Unfortunately, his passionate enthusiasm did not always issue quite as pleasantly. He was 36 when, at a ball at Bath, he caught sight of Julia Thuillier— "a glorious creature with wonderful golden hair." "By heaven," he exclaimed, before he had even spoken to her, "I'll marry her!" And he did, almost immediately, but it ended miserably, as it was bound to do.

Another of his stormy impulses sent him rushing off to the Peninsula, to fight under the Duke against Napoleon, at the head of a regiment that he had himself recruited and financed. But, in war as in love, he was a blunderer, and the thing was a fiasco. Yet, while these incidental and subsidiary enthusiasms petered out, the supreme enthusiasm of his life, his passion for pure English, waxed rather than waned with the years. As a result he won for himself, as Swinburne puts it, such a double crown of glory, in verse and in prose, as has been won by no other Englishman but Milton. Landor sleeps under the cypresses in the picturesque little cemetery just outside the walls of Florence. Hard by are the tombs of Arthur Hugh Clough, Theodore Parker, and Elizabeth Barrett Browning, and, leaving him in such excellent company, we gratefully salute him.

An Unpredictable Scientist

It is exactly a hundred years since articles first appeared in the English magazines by a writer who was destined to become famous as the most delightful and entertaining naturalist of all time.

As a small boy, Frank Buckland, the son of a renowned geologist, betrayed an extraordinary understanding of animals. If alive, he adopted them; if dead, he devoured them; and, if they were both dead and buried, he exhumed them. When his grave and reverent seniors protested against his eating such nasty fare, he asked how they knew it was nasty if they had never tried it.

When he slept with other boys in camp or dormitory, he would awaken his companions at midnight, and, their nostrils having been assailed by a savory smell, he would regale them with grilled mice which, he assured them, were far tastier than larks. Squirrel pie, roast viper, and frogs in batter were often included in his menu.

And, even in his mature days, he would entertain his guests with elephant soup, giraffe steak, panther chops or a tasty dish of alligator. He sometimes admitted that, the creature having reposed for too long in its grave at the zoo, the meal was not quite so toothsome as he had hoped.

Projected Human Mind into Animal Conditions

At school, unsympathetic masters objected to his stuffing his desk with animals which, though long dead, made their presence unpleasantly perceptible. He surmounted this difficulty by ingratiating himself in the affections of the bellringer at the church, who allowed him to take his deceased friends to the top of the tower and to leave them there until the bleached skeletons could be added, without odoriferous offence, to his museum.

His home swarmed with his weird pets. His wife used to say that, instead of marrying a man, she had inadvertently married a menagerie. His neighbors dreaded the delivery of his daily mail. They never knew what might escape from the odd looking packages in the postman's bag.

The greatest day of his life was the day on which he became an angler. He took to fishing as some men take to drinking, and soon became gloriously intoxicated. He could talk of nothing but lines and hooks and casts and flies. He often declared that the greatest thrill that he ever experienced was the landing of his first salmon. The inevitable happened; he fell in love with the fish. He studied their haunts and habits so intently that he came to feel as if in some earlier incarnation, he had himself been a salmon and had retained a vivid memory of a salmon's sensations, difficulties, and requirements. Although a qualified surgeon, he was appointed Inspector of British Fisheries, and some of his reports are still regarded as classics of their kind.

Exploring a Realm of Peril and Wonder

He will always be remembered for his invention of the water ladder, a contrivance by means of which fish could climb a weir and pass on upstream. When the pontiffs ridiculed his suggestion, his reply was unanswerable. "Build an inexpensive ladder," he pleaded, "and leave the ultimate decision to the salmon." The temporary structure was erected and the salmon voted unanimously for Buckland.

His investigations were often beset by peril. In taking from the cobra's cage at the zoo a rat that had been bitten by the reptile, the venom passed through a scratch on his finger into his own system. Before he left the gardens, he was staggering like a drunken man; he was rushed to hospital and hovered for some time at death's door. On another occasion, he maddened a viper until it bit savagely at the glass slide that he held in his hand. Examining the resultant drops under a powerful microscope, he said that their coruscations and crystallisations reminded him of the flashing of the aurora borealis.

Endowed with a most charming personality, he won the confidence and friendship of many of the most eminent men of his time. His home life was idyllic. And, by means of a fluent and natural style, he secured the admiration and even affection of millions of readers. He died at 54, confident that his most exciting discoveries were yet to be made. "God is so very good to the little fishes," he said, "that He will never allow their inspector to suffer shipwreck at the last!" His books are still being issued in the popular libraries and a monument to his memory is to be seen at South Kensington.

First Across Australia

I t was on 21 February, 1861, that Burke and Wills and King and Gray, having pioneered the crossing of the Australian continent, turned their faces southward for the tragic journey home. Beyond the shadow of a doubt the Burke and Wills expedition that, having achieved its end so triumphantly, nevertheless perished so lamentably, was one of the most perfectly-equipped expeditions that ever plunged into the interior of a continent. No expense was spared to ensure its unqualified success. Twenty-six camels were specially imported from India. The men were attended by a long procession of horses and drays and furnished with 21 tons of provisions and paraphernalia. When we remember that Eyre crossed the southern desert and reached West Australia in safety, with all his equipment on his shoulder, it seems an irony of circumstance that these brave men, so liberally furnished, should have died of starvation.

The story of the expedition is one long chapter of blunders. But all those blunders are, in reality, comprehended in one initial blunder—the appointment of a leader. Robert O'Hara Burke was a very brave man, cool, fearless, uncomplaining, and indomitable. As a follower he would have been all that the most exacting commander could desire. But he lacked the first essentials of leadership. He was impatient, impulsive, and unwilling to consider the suggestions of his comrades; he failed most deplorably to win the confidence of those who followed him; he quarreled with loyal companions on petty issues; he so promoted and so punished his men as to awaken suspicion and distrust; and his vacillating decisions were invariably wrong. It is easy to be wise after the event, but nobody can peruse the records without occasionally speculating on the possibilities of the situation had Burke died at Coopers Creek on the outward journey instead of on the homeward one, and had Wills succeeded to the command.

Expedition Wrecked by Errors of Judgment

William John Wills was a very gallant gentleman. He was only 26, but he was a student, athlete, competent astronomer, and wise beyond his years. His charming and magnetic personality led the authorities, despite his youth, to appoint him third in command. Landels was second, but Landels and his leader soon quarreled and Wills was promoted to the vacant place. Over and over again, in the course of that memorable journey, decisions had to be made on which, as it turned out, the fate of the party depended. If on any one of those crucial occasions, Burke had accepted the advice of Wills, the expedition would have returned in safety. But Burke rejected the counsel of his brilliant young colleague, relied—as his duty was—on his own judgment, and the party perished. Perhaps the very modesty of Wills unfitted him for the stern tasks of leadership, and, in any case, there is small profit in dwelling on the might-have-beens of history. The thing has happened and we must take it as it stands.

Yet, for all that, there are few incidents in the world's history that suggest more futile wishes than does that epic story we recall with pride today. If only Burke had waited until he was ready, instead of setting out with one section of his party, leaving the other to follow later! Waiting was inevitable, but waiting in the desert instead of in Melbourne meant devouring during idle days the provisions that were so precious. Again, if only, having made such an arrangement, he had stuck to it and remained at Coopers Creek until his rearguard arrived! Or, since the plan was to be changed, if only Burke and his three companions had set out on their dash to the North a few days earlier! If only, on their return, they had hurried back to Coopers Creek instead of pausing for 24 hours beside the grave of Gray! In either of these events the party that crossed the continent would have reached the stockade before Brahe and his men had evacuated it. As it was, Burke, Wills and King arrived back only seven hours too late.

Toll for the Brave that are No More

Again, if only, as Wills urged, they had immediately followed Brahe, or waited for a day or two at Coopers Creek, or at the very least, left some clear evidence at Coopers Creek to show they had returned to the depot! For Brahe, a few miles out from Coopers Creek had met the long-delayed rearguard; he then led the entire party back to the familiar camping ground, but failed to notice on his return to it, that the lost explorers had during his short absence, visited the spot. Burke, in the teeth of Wills' entreaties, had decided to strike across country to Adelaide. He argued that, with his exhausted camels, he could not hope to overtake Brahe with his fresh ones. Towards Adelaide they turned their faces and staggered out into the desert to their deaths.

Near Parliament House, Melbourne, there stands a noble monument to the memory of these valiant men. It was the first piece of statuary of which the city could boast, and stood in the center of Collins St. until the exigencies of traffic drove it farther out. It represents the eager Burke, his hand resting on the shoulder of his young lieutenant, shading his eyes with his hand as he scans the distant skyline, while Wills is making an entry in his journal. The bas-reliefs depict: (1) The starting of the expedition from Royal Park; (2) the terrible return to the deserted camp; (3) the blacks weeping over the dead body of Burke; (4) the finding of King by the relief expedition. It is a story so full of attractiveness, splendor, and pathos that we in Australia must always regard it as an integral part of our national heritage.

Imagination and Science

At the age of 20, Jules Verne burst upon Paris. For years he had cherished romantic dreams of tasting the bohemian life of the capital. He arrived to find the city in the throes of revolution. Blood was flowing in the streets; paving stones were being torn up to build barricades; the king was being bundled off the throne.

Bewildered and dumbfounded, Jules Verne felt as a man might feel who, having accepted an invitation to stay with a relative, reaches the house just as his host, in a fit of drunken fury, is smashing the windows and setting fire to the furniture.

Five years later, Paris having regained her sanity, one might meet, on the Champs Elysses, a young dandy of striking, open face, with curly hair falling about his massive forehead. He wears an immaculate velvet jacket and an elaborate bow tie. As a law student, he has become fond of Paris and has written a sheaf of trifles, including daring flights of fancy, modeled partly on Alexandre Dumas and partly on Edgar Allan Poe. For Jules Verne has not yet found Jules Verne.

Various Professions as Stepping Stones to Fame

Three years later, to the consternation of his father, he relinquished his legal studies and became a stockbroker. Two considerations dictated the change. Desperately anxious to marry, he needed money, and he thought that he could achieve wealth more swiftly on the Stock Exchange than in chambers. And he fancies that the new vocation will give him more time for literary enterprise.

As a matter of fact, his application to the law and his devotion to the Stock Exchange were, both of them, harmless flirtations. At heart he was neither barrister nor stockbroker. He aimed at authorship, and, the moment that he had attained that elevation, he was resolved to throw down the ladder by which he had climbed.

He had to wait six long years. After a few months as a stockbroker he had realized the first of his dreams; he married his beloved Honorine. And then he set to work to attain his second goal. He rose at five every morning, snatched something from the pantry, rushed to his desk, and wrote frantically for five hours. Then, at ten o'clock, Jules Verne the Visionary became magically transformed into Jules Verne the Stockbroker, and, a city person to the last bootlace, he set off for the office.

An Eager Prospector Strikes Gold at Last

It was in 1863, at the age of 35, that he found his metier. It was the age of the balloon. Fugitive ascents had often been made in the course of the centuries; but, at that time, Glaisher was experimenting on behalf of the British Association, reaching on one occasion an altitude of 37,000 feet.

Giving rein to his fancy, Jules Verne exploited the passion of the period. He published his *Five Weeks in a Balloon* and felt in his very bones that he had pegged his claim to world-wide renown.

When his publisher congratulated him on his triumph, the young author startled him by reeling off the plots of a dozen highly imaginative novels stacked away amidst the gray matter of his fertile brain. He was as excited as a schoolboy. While the mood was upon him, he called together his friends on the Bourse. "I am leaving you," he cried to the astonished stockbrokers. "I have written a novel of an entirely new kind. If it succeeds, it will be a gold mine. I shall go on writing without a break, while you continue to buy shares the day before they slump, and sell them the day before they soar! Goodbye!" That speech marked the birth of Jules Verne as the world knows him.

He traveled in order that his oceans of fancy might be studded with picturesque islands of fact. By introducing into his weird narratives actual descriptions of real places, he provided, as Pooh Bah would say, some corroborative detail, designed to give artistic verisimilitude to an otherwise unconvincing narrative. But the excursions of his body were mere evening strolls compared with the excursions of his brain. He liked to set his plots in places that no human eye had ever beheld; amidst such scenes he was immune from contradiction. In graphically portraying the center of the earth, the bed of the ocean, and the surface of the moon he could let himself go; he had invaded a realm that was exclusively his own.

Keeping himself abreast of the science of his time, he allowed his vivid imagination to go just one step ahead. He regarded each sensational invention as embryonic; it foretold a still greater wonder. For this reason, there was something prophetic about him; many of his wildest imaginings were but the shadows of things to come. Nursed by his faithful Honorine, he died in the early morning of a perfect spring day in 1905. He was then 77. Four days later, 5,000 people, including troops of school children who had devoured every line that he had written, followed him to his grave.

Possibility Thinker

In the most modest and unpretentious circumstances, Thomas Alva Edison was born in Ohio on February 11, 1847. He was scarcely out of his cradle when he formed the conviction that nothing thinkable is impossible; and, at the age of eighty-four, he died translating into concrete actualities the wildest and weirdest conceptions of his restless brain. Multitudinous and bewildering as were his countless inventions, it is impossible to lay down the list of his countless and almost incredible triumphs without feeling that the mind that could wrestle with such problems, and produce such wonders, was itself, far and away, the most miraculous piece of mechanism of them all.

Like Faraday, on whom, to some extent, he modeled his career, he owed practically nothing to his education. He spent three months at school. His mother, and his own sharp eyes, taught him all that he came to know. Having once learned to read, he felt that the world was at his feet. As a small boy he devoured the entire contents of an encyclopedia, Hume's *History of England*, Gibbon's *Decline and Fall*, Newton's *Principia*, and he one day entered the Public Library at Detroit with the avowed intention of absorbing the entire contents of the institution, book by book! Every experience that came his way became grist to his mill. He began life by selling newspapers and fruit on a railway train. He was soon printing a paper of his own on that selfsame train. A little later, to further some of his other experiments, he added a laboratory to his traveling equipment; had the misfortune to set the van on fire; was severely cuffed by the angry guard; and the blow burdened him with lifelong deafness.

Touching Life at a Thousand Points

The precise number of his inventions will never be known. More than a thousand of his amazing contrivances were patented in the United States alone. In his 24th year he had 45 distinct inventions simultaneously under way, and the Patent Commissioner described him as "the young man who keeps the path to the Patents Office hot with his footsteps." He allowed no grass to grow under his feet. At four o'clock one afternoon he made an important discovery; he immediately rushed to his solicitor, who instantly cabled particulars to London; and, next day, he was informed that his idea was under serious consideration in England. In an essay on Edison, Mr. Lionel Elvin remarks that he himself is writing on a typewriter by the light of an incandescent electric lamp. The room contains a gramophone, a wireless set and a telephone. As soon as his manuscript is complete, he intends to ring up a cinema to reserve seats for the evening. He will find his way to the theater by electric train and then go home by taxi. And for all these things—the typewriter, the lamp, the gramophone, the radio, the telephone, the moving pictures, the electric train and the automobile—he is indebted to Edison.

Thomas Edison represents in his own person the new trend in scientific thought. More than three centuries ago, Lord Bacon hurled the thunderbolts of his vigorous denunciation into the academies of the scientists and the portals of the philosophers, charging these learned speculators with making no real contribution to the practical welfare of the race. "Words, and more words, and nothing but words," he complained, "has been the fruit of the toil of the most renowned sages of sixty generations." The old philosophy had been singularly shy of meddling in matters that might serve some utilitarian end, lest it should be supposed that academic pursuits were simply followed for the sake of the vulgar purposes that they promoted.

Science Looks at Life, Transfigures Everything

For many hundreds of years the most capable thinkers were content to deal in nebulous theories, abstract speculations, mystifying hypotheses and occult disquisitions. Science was in the world like a spider in the water, with its own native atmosphere gathered closely about it and fearful lest any general admixture should take place between the element that was the breath of its own nostrils and the turbid body of affairs beyond it. Even Seneca ridiculed the thinkers who applied their powers to increasing the comfort of their homes. "The invention of such appliances," he said, "is drudgery for the lowest slaves; philosophy lies deeper. It is not for her to teach men how to use their hands; her mission is to form the soul." It was against this pernicious doctrine that, in season and out of season Bacon protested. And with good effect. In a telling essay Macaulay has shown how Bacon's gospel transfigured civilization. It has lengthened human life, he says; has mitigated pain; has extinguished diseases; has increased the fertility of the soil; it has given new security to shipping; has spanned huge rivers, has guided the thunderbolt innocuously from heaven to earth; has lighted up the night with the splendor of the day; has extended the range of human vision, has multiplied the power of the human muscles; has accelerated motion; has annihilated distance; has facilitated intercourse; has enabled man to descend into the depths of the sea; to soar into the sky, to penetrate the noxious recesses of the earth; and to traverse land, sea and air at incredible rates of speed. In this cavalcade of achievement, no one scientist has played a braver part than Thomas Alva Edison. One of the most impressive pages of the New Testament describes the way in which the scientists of an earlier day laid their tributes of gold and frankincense and myrrh at the divine feet. Lives like those of Faraday and Edison prove that, when that act of adoration has once been sincerely performed, science turns from the presence of Deity to the service of Humanity, transforming every phase of human experience in the process.

Sweetness and Light

Among writers of our time, is there one to whom we feel more deeply indebted than to John Galsworthy? To have read the *Forsyth Saga* is to have imbibed a liberal education, not only in letters but in life.

Galsworthy was one of the most magnetic and most dynamic figures of the years between the two wars. Rather above medium height, of well-proportioned and well-built frame, finely-chiseled face, kindly welcoming eyes, and possessing a voice that, though resonant and strong, was almost caressing in its softness, John Galsworthy, by his presence, gave an air of distinction to every circle in which he moved. He was, in the best sense of the term, the perfect gentlemen. He looked a gentleman; he spoke as a gentleman; he dressed as a gentleman; he behaved as a gentleman; he felt and thought as a gentleman; he was a gentleman.

He excelled in the gentleman's delicate art of putting his companion—whoever his companion might happen to be—delightfully at ease. He overawed nobody. In chatting with kings or with cabmen he was always himself. He never put on airs or stood upon his dignity.

The most celebrated men and women of his time reveled in his society. Little children, of whom he had none of his own, thought it as good as a holiday when he led their frolics or told them stories. His wife, even in sickness, found him the gentlest and most skillful of nurses, praising his velvety hands, while his horses and his dogs seemed to worship the ground he trod.

It was his wife who made an author of him. He had always longed to do such work, but felt it to be hopelessly beyond him. "Why don't you write? You're just the person!" exclaimed the girl whom he afterwards married. Galsworthy, who by this time had been called to the Bar, regarded the words as a challenge. He relinquished his chambers, announced that he had embraced literature as a profession, and settled down to write his first book.

Reaching Heights after Haunting Hollows

His first ventures by no means set the Thames on fire. They were kindly, though not enthusiastically, received; and the sales were fair. And then, having hovered uncertainly for nearly 10 years between the misty levels of mediocrity and the sunlit uplands of actual brilliance, John Galsworthy, in 1906, at the age of 39, produced the work that established him as one of the great masters. In that memorable year he published

The Man of Property, the first volume of the famous *Saga*, and also produced *The Silver Box*, the first of his plays.

Galsworthy approached his 40th birthday with the pleasing consciousness that he had taken his place as one of the brightest stars in the literary firmament of his time. Men recognized that, in him they had an author who walked very closely with life. He was neither a dreamy idealist nor a vulgar realist. In all his novels and plays he submitted his characters to one acid test: Do men and women in real life talk and dress and behave like this?

He had no patience with figures in fiction who spend their time in making elaborate speeches to each other. Queen Victoria once complained that Mr. Gladstone addressed her as if she were a public meeting. The heroes and heroines of the old-fashioned novels had a similar ugly habit. John Galsworthy detested it, and determined to set a happier fashion.

Literature, so far as his work was concerned, should be a mirror held to the face of life. His men and women should be the sort of men and women whom one meets in banks and shops and restaurants and picture-shows and railway trains—ordinary but interesting, commonplace but lovable.

Inspired Himself, Galsworthy Inspires Others

John Galsworthy, who refused a knighthood, shares with Sir Hugh Walpole the distinction of having restored the massive and monumental novel to popular favor. "With all my heart," Walpole wrote to Galsworthy, "I congratulate you on bringing to completion so great a work. What a triumph to have created something that really beautifies the world and will go on doing so! You do not realize what a help your quietness and dignity are to many of us. The temptations to be cheap and nasty are now legion, and one has to hold on for dear life. When I hesitate I always think of you and you help me marvellously." It is not too much to say that, in these telling sentences, Sir Hugh Walpole spoke for all the writers of his time.

Galsworthy never moralized nor sermonized; yet, to him, his work was but a means to an end. The dominant passion of his life was to ameliorate the condition of all things that suffered. He labored tirelessly to introduce mercy into slaughter-houses, to prevent vivisection of dogs, to remove ponies from the mines, and to open the cages of all wild birds. His play *Justice*, revealed to Mr. Churchill, and to the public, the horrors of solitary confinement and led to a sensational reform in the treatment of prisoners.

Galsworthy made money at a prodigious rate, but he distributed it with a princely hand. On the day on which he received the Nobel Prize of £9,000 he gave away the entire amount. During the First World War he worked early and late, donating all his earnings to national funds. Mr. H. V. Marrat, who knew him intimately, declares that his outstanding characteristic was "an uncommon sweetness." By his masterly and masculine writings, John Galsworthy contrived to infuse the winsomeness and beauty of his own soul into the life and thought of the English people.

The Integrity of Science

Charles Darwin was only 22 when, through the influence of his old teacher, Prof. J. S. Henslow, he was invited to set out on a five-year cruise as naturalist without pay on H.M.S. Beagle. The tall young student's first reactions to the novel idea were by no means favorable. He eyed the project dubiously. Few ambitious youths of 22 lightly forgo, for five long years, the opportunity of earning money. But, the longer he pondered it, the more attractive the adventure seemed, and he finished up by accepting the invitation with schoolboy enthusiasm. To the last day of his long and useful life he congratulated himself on that decision. "The voyage of the Beagle," he would tell his friends, "stands out as the most important event in my life; it determined my whole career." Moreover, it enriched our literature with several volumes, the direct outcome of observations made in the course of the tour.

In addition to *The Voyage of the Beagle*, one of the most fascinating and informative travel stories ever penned, the enterprise led also to the writing of *The Zoology of the Beagle* and other masterpieces.

The *Quarterly Review* said of *The Voyage of the Beagle* that it contains ample material for deep thinking; it abounds in the vivid description that fills the mind's eye with brighter pictures than any painter can present; while it is marked by the charm arising from the freshness of heart which is thrown over these virgin pages by a strong intellectual man and an acute and profound observer.

The Whole Truth, and Nothing but the Truth

Prof. J. A. Thomson defines the scientific temper as consisting of three cardinal and fundamental virtues. A man must have, he says, a clear and unbiased vision; he must exhibit a caution that can never be marred by impatience to reach a conclusion; and he must possess a genuine passion for facts. Huxley spoke of "that enthusiasm for truth, that fanaticism of veracity, which is a greater treasure than much learning, a nobler gift than the power of increasing knowledge." It is to the everlasting credit of the world of science that it has frequently produced monumental examples of this intellectual chastity; but, among those illustrious names, there is none that, in the sheer transparency of his soul and in his absolute loyalty to his vision, shines with a brighter luster than Darwin's.

With Darwin, honesty was an instinct. In his earliest autobiographical records he tells the stark truth about himself with brutal candor. One of his sons, Sir Francis Darwin, as a small boy, once asked his father, in the presence of a number of famous men and women, if he was ever tipsy. Most men so situated would have hedged, prevaricated, or turned the question aside as a joke. But not Darwin. "I am ashamed to say that I once was—at Cambridge," he replied, with characteristic frankness and circumstantial exactitude. Sir Francis Darwin confesses, in his biography of his renowned sire, that the stark veracity and crystalline honesty of that straightforward answer made an indelible impression on his own childish mind. Once as a boy, Darwin pitilessly thrashed a puppy. He was moved to this act of tyranny by the sheer exuberance of power. He was the master; the puppy was his slave. A minute later he felt thoroughly ashamed. In the ordinary way, the incident would have passed into oblivion. But Darwin felt that the man who writes an autobiography must tell the whole truth: and he therefore pillories himself for all the world to see.

Does the Exception Prove the Rule?

This admirable trait marked all his researches. Through long years of patient investigation, Darwin would discover that thousands of specimens in given circumstances behave in a particular way. The evidence would appear overwhelming; but just as he was about to generalize on these harmonious observations, and to announce the confident conclusion to which all the facts so steadily pointed, he would suddenly come upon a specimen that, under identically similar conditions, behaved in a radically different way. It would have been the easiest thing in the world to have dismissed the recalcitrant phenomenon with the cheap sophistry that the exception proves the rule. But so plausible a way of escape is inconsistent with the best traditions of science; and Darwin, with impeccable fidelity to truth, immediately abandoned the premature conclusion as untenable. "The little beast is doing just what I did not want him do," Darwin would exclaim, and, without a moment's delay, he would evacuate the position to which years of research had led him.

One evening towards the end, Darwin entertained Prof. G. J. Romanes at his Kentish home. His son, Sir Francis Darwin, was also present. The conversation, turning to the ability of magnificent scenery to awaken emotions of reverence, Darwin casually remarked that he had never experienced that sensation so powerfully as when standing on the slopes of the Cordilleras. Shortly afterwards he retired for the night. But a couple of hours later, clad in dressing-gown and slippers, he reappeared to tell the two younger men, who were still lingering beside the fire, that he had unwittingly misled them. "It was in the forests of Brazil," he said, "and not among the Cordilleras, that I was most overcome by the sensation of reverence. I could not sleep until I had corrected myself. It might conceivably affect your conclusions." It was a small thing, a mere matter of personal taste and sentiment; but the old man, true to the last to the finest traditions of the scientific temper, felt that his memory had betrayed him into a position from which he must frankly and openly withdraw. There, as in a cameo, is reflected both the spirit of Charles Darwin and the spirit of all true science.

Volumes of Splendor

The sixteenth of January is the anniversary of the death of the greatest historian of all time. Edward Gibbon died on Jan. 16, 1794. Nobody who knew him in the days immediately preceding his epoch-making achievement dreamed for a single moment that he had it in him to write a masterpiece that mankind would prize for centuries. Looking for all the world like a thorough-paced fop, a beau, a dancing-master, he has been described by so many of his illustrious contemporaries that we all seem to have seen him.

He is a podgy figure dressed in an elaborate suit of flowered velvet with silk stockings and silver buckles. The gay kerchief that he so ostentatiously flutters, and the gold snuffbox that he so frequently taps, stamp him as one of the dandies of the town. Painfully self-conscious, he is a creature of quickly-moving hands, of restless, nervous eyes, of fair hair faultlessly arranged and delicately powdered, of depressed nose and huge protuberant cheeks. It seems hard on one who is so extremely anxious to cut a handsome figure in society that Nature has done so little to promote this end. Over such handicaps, however, he triumphed gloriously. His *Decline and Fall of the Roman Empire* is the greatest history ever written. It set a new fashion in the craft of the chronicler. Instead of merely raking among dead men's bones, Gibbon electrified antiquity, making the cobwebbed and moth-eaten past live throbbingly again. His glowing and interminable panorama is indescribable. Every chapter seems to be a more gorgeous painting on a more spacious canvas than the one that preceded it. The imagination is captivated by the swaying hordes of Goths and Huns, Vandals and Saracens; the imposing and variegated pageant of martial movement sweeps majestically through one's mind for weeks after laying the volumes aside. It is archaeology palpitating with vitality.

Summoning the Glorious Ghosts of Yesterday

With that characteristic egotism which, in the perspective of history, we find so intriguing, Gibbon has told us of the circumstances and emotions that marked alike the conception, and the completion of his magnum opus. It was on Oct. 15, 1764, that as a young man of 27, the idea of becoming the historian of a fallen empire first captivated his fancy. On a holiday visit to Rome he stood for the first time among the ruins of the Capitol. As he watched the bare-footed friars chanting vespers in the Temple of Jupiter, the splendid specters of long-forgotten centuries seemed to fill the air, challenging him to give them corporeal life once more.

It was on June 27, 1787, that he finished his stupendous task. He was then 50. In a postscript which he appends to his manuscript, he describes the tumult of emotion with which, after so many years of closest application, he penned the last line of the last volume. It was a radiant midsummer night at Lausanne. "After laying down my pen," he says, "I took several turns in a covered walk of acacias which commanded a prospect of the country, the lake and the mountains. The air was temperate, the sky was serene, the silver orb of the moon was reflected from the waters and all nature was silent." He sighs with relief at having regained his freedom: he feels a lump in his throat as he takes farewell of a work that has been, through all his mature years, his constant companion. Between those two dates—1764 and 1787—we catch fitful and fugitive glimpses of him as, with the romances and the tragedies of a score of empires exciting his fevered brain, he haunts the libraries, the coffee-houses and the clubrooms of London.

A Proud Citizen of a Score of Centuries

Gibbon was a familiar figure in that famous circle that revolved about the colossal and commanding personality of Dr. Samuel Johnson—the circle that included Sir Joshua Reynolds, David Garrick, Edmund Burke, Oliver Goldsmith, James Boswell, and all the rest of them. He entered Parliament in 1774, although he never once addressed the House. He was known to have a lodging, overflowing with stacks of historical tomes, in Bentinck St., Manchester Square, in the seclusion of which he forsook the eighteenth century and rambled at will among all the others. He several times heard Dr. Johnson declare that the artistry of history was an unconquered realm. It was all an affair of dates and kings and battles: nobody had ever written a history as a history should be written. Gibbon thought of the manuscript lying on his desk at Manchester Square and secretly vowed that he would remove that reproach. And, as everybody knows, he did it.

He lived for nearly seven years after finishing his masterpiece. His closing days were brightened by the conviction that he was recognized as the greatest historian of all time. For, first and last, he was essentially an egotist. Edward Gibbon believed implicitly in Edward Gibbon. He never asked advice: he never conferred with others: he never showed a sentence to anybody until it was published. His work is one of the wonders of the world. He ransacked the archives of 50 nations and caught the spirit of 20 separate centuries. With the most serene confidence he leads across his glowing pages the colorful procession of the ancient Orient and the stately drama of modern Europe. His theme, however stupendous, is always well within his grasp. He moves through the ages with the tramp of a conqueror. We may smile at the foppish little coxcomb as, in his dainty suit, he lounges in the corner of some odorous tavern, tiresomely tapping that golden snuffbox; we may be amused at the importance that he attaches to his own sayings and his own doings; but, for all that, we are compeled to admire his titanic achievement and to salute him as one of the greatest masters of our English speech.

About the Cover

Nuggets bring to mind gold but our title, *Nuggets of Romance*, has more to do with the wonders in life, the surprises that bring delight and awe. They are found along the way by people like F. W. Boreham. Their senses have been exercised to notice and pay attention. We do well to follow their example.

A pile of gold pieces lost out to rocks glistening from a stream bed, which is a more natural setting. The surreal colors make them like nuggets flashing their brilliance. It reminds me of how God takes a heart of stone and makes it a heart of flesh. As shown in the book, God works through all sorts of people in wildly imaginative ways. It is astonishing that He condescends to use us at all.

I hope the cover conveys a little of the surprise and inspiration found in the book. May this volume leave you marveling at the gracious gifts that God gives so freely. This is the romance of wonder.

Michael Dalton

Publisher's Note

We are grateful to Dr. Frank Rees at Whitley College
for the permission to publish this book and for the
practical support given by the College.

A portion of the sale of each book will go toward
the training of pastors and missionaries at
Whitley College, a ministry that
F. W. Boreham supported during his lifetime.

Sincere thanks to Laura Zugzda for cover design
and Marcia Breece for layout.

Further information about the life and work of
F. W. Boreham is available at the F. W. Boreham
Facebook page: http://www.facebook.com/pages/F-W-
Boreham/121475236386.

Please address any comments and questions to:

Geoff Pound
24 Montana Street
GLEN IRIS
Australia 3146
+61 (0) 417 485200
geoffpound@gmail.com

Jeff Cranston
LowCountry Community Church
801 Buckwalter Parkway
Bluffton, SC 29910
jcranston@lowcountrycc.org
www.lowcountrycc.org

Michael Dalton
2163 Fern Street
Eureka, CA 95503
(707) 442-8967
dalton.michael@sbcglobal.net

We enjoy hearing from people. Let us know if you have
benefited from this or any of our other publications.

CPSIA information can be obtained
at www.ICGtesting.com
Printed in the USA
LVHW091944170720
660992LV00006B/609

9 780983 287551